HOW CHILDREN DISCOVER NEW STRATEGIES

HOW CHILDREN DISCOVER NEW STRATEGIES

Robert S. Siegler
Eric Jenkins
Carnegie-Mellon University

LEA *LAWRENCE ERLBAUM ASSOCIATES, PUBLISHERS*

1989 *Hillsdale, New Jersey* *Hove and London*

Lawrence Erlbaum Associates, Inc., Publishers
365 Broadway
Hillsdale, New Jersey 07642

Library of Congress Cataloging-in-Publication Data
Siegler, Robert S.
    How children discover new strategies / Robert S. Siegler, Eric A.
Jenkins.
        p.   cm. — (John M. MacEachran memorial lecture series)
    Includes index.
    ISBN 0-8058-0472-2
    1. Cognition in children.   2. Problem solving in children.
I. Jenkins, Eric A.   II. Title.   III. Series.
BF723.C5S553   1989
155.4'13 — dc20   89-2658
                                                                CIP

Printed in the United States of America
10 9 8 7 6 5 4 3 2

To *Todd, Beth,* and *Aaron Siegler*
and *Rosemary* and *Eric Jenkins, Sr.,*
from whom we have learned much

Contents

Preface

In October of 1987 I received a phone call from Jeff Bisanz inviting me to present the 14th Annual MacEachran Lectures at the University of Alberta. Illustrious predecessors, freedom to pursue any set of issues, and an attentive audience were among the attractions he cited. The opportunity seemed too good to pass up.

In October of 1988, almost exactly 1 year later, I spent a most enjoyable week in Edmonton presenting a series of three lectures. What made the experience so enjoyable was not only the exceptional warmth and hospitality that I was shown, but also the remarkable prior preparation of so many members of the intellectual community. People had read, thought about, and discussed my work, so that they were deeply knowledgeable about it even before I came. This allowed me to cover basic background material quickly and to focus on the questions and issues that were in the forefront of my own thinking. It was an altogether rare experience and one to be savored.

In our initial conversation, Jeff suggested that I might wish to talk about the recent work that Eric Jenkins and I were doing on how children discover new strategies. In the previous 5 years, my research had focused on how children choose among strategies that they already know. The new research addressed the complementary question of how children discover new strategies in the first place. Because Eric and I had not written about this work previously, we decided to make it the focus of this volume.

The investigations of strategy discovery are in some ways for me a synthesis of old and new research programs. Much of my earlier research using the rule assessment approach examined how children progress from using a less advanced rule to using a more advanced one on balance scale, projection of shadows, probability, conservation, and other problems. My more recent work has focused on situations such as arithmetic, time telling, spelling, and reading in which individual children know and use multiple strategies, and in which much of development involves a shift in the relative frequency of existing strategies, rather than a shift from one strategy to a different one. Even in domains where children already possess multiple strategies, however, they also discover new ones. It is here that the new research meets the old.

Although both the previous and current research concern acquisition of new strategies, there are also important differences between the two. These reflect the greater complexity of analyzing situations in which children use multiple strategies rather than a single one, and also the use of more sensitive methods that allow trial-by-trial identification of the strategy that a given child used on each problem. Such trial-by-trial identification proved to be critical to the present investigation, because it allowed identification of the exact point at which each child discovered the new strategy. This identification, in turn, made possible the examination of the circumstances leading up to the discovery and examination of how children generalized the strategy beyond its initial use. The nature of the initial discovery, the circumstances leading up to it, and the generalization of the strategy to new problems were the central topics of the present research.

ACKNOWLEDGMENTS

We have many people to thank, both in Edmonton and in Pittsburgh, for making the book possible. Gay and Jeff Bisanz and Gene Lechelt were more-than-generous hosts. They and JoAnn LeFevre, Fred Morrison, Ed Cornell, Don Heth, Rene Elio, Peter Dixon, and Alinda Friedman were some of the many people at Alberta who offered valuable comments on the research. Jeff Shrager, and especially Dave

Klahr and Jim Staszewski were among the Pittsburgh family who made valuable contributions. Others worthy of special mention are Daniella Cramer, who, along with the second author, served as experimenter in the study, Darlene Scalese who, in addition to doing a large amount of typing, always did whatever it took to get the job done, and the teachers and administrators of the Carnegie Mellon Children's school, including Ann Taylor, Jean Veltri, Jean Bird, Rita Devlin, Ron Fricke, Judy Hallinen, and Theresa Jankowski. They all assisted above and beyond the call of duty. Of course, the most special thanks go to the children. All of their help was invaluable.

Robert S. Siegler

JOHN M. MacEACHRAN MEMORIAL LECTURE SERIES

The Department of Psychology at the University of Alberta inaugurated the MacEachran Memorial Lecture Series in 1975 in honor of the late Professor John M. MacEachran. Professor MacEachran was born in Ontario in 1877 and received a Ph.D. in Philosophy from Queen's University in 1905. In 1906 he left for Germany to begin more formal study in psychology, first spending just less than a year in Berlin with Stumpf, and then moving to Leipzig, where he completed a second Ph.D. in 1908 with Wundt as his supervisor. During this period he also spent time in Paris studying under Durkheim and Henri Bergson. With these impressive qualifications the University of Alberta was particularly fortunate in attracting him to its faculty in 1909.

Professor MacEachran's impact has been significant at the university, provincial, and national levels. At the University of Alberta he offered the first courses in psychology and subsequently served as Head of the Department of Philosophy and Psychology and Provost of the University until his retirement in 1945. It was largely owing to his activities and example that several areas of academic study were established on a firm and enduring basis. In addition to playing a major role in establishing the Faculties of Medicine, Education and Law in this Province, Professor MacEachran was also instrumental in the formative stages of the Mental Health Movement in Alberta. At a national level, he was one of the founders of the Canadian Psychological Association and also became its first Honorary President in 1939. John M. MacEachran was indeed one of the pioneers in the development of psychology in Canada.

Perhaps the most significant aspect of the MacEachran Memorial Lecture Series has been the continuing agreement that the Department of Psychology at the University of Alberta has with Lawrence Erlbaum Associates, Publishers, Inc., for the publication of each lecture series. The following is a list of the Invited Speakers and the titles of their published lectures:

1975   Frank A. Geldard (Princeton University)
           "Sensory Saltation: Metastability in the Perceptual World"

1976   Benton J. Underwood (Northwestern University)
           "Temporal Codes for Memories: Issues and Problems"

1977   David Elkind (Rochester University)
           "The Child's Reality: Three Developmental Themes"

1978   Harold Kelley (University of California at Los Angeles)
           "Personal Relationships: Their Structures and Processes"

1979   Robert Rescorla (Yale University)
        "Pavlovian Second-Order Conditioning:
        Studies in Associative Learning"

1980   Mortimer Mishkin (NIMH-Bethesda)
        "Cognitive Circuits" (*unpublished*)

1981   James Greeno (University of Pittsburgh)
        "Current Cognitive Theory in Problem Solving" (*unpublished*)

1982   William Uttal (University of Michigan)
        "Visual Form Detection in 3-Dimensional Space"

1983   Jean Mandler (University of California at San Diego)
        "Stories, Scripts, and Scenes: Aspects of Schema Theory"

1984   George Collier and Carolyn Rovee-Collier
           (Rutgers University)
        "Learning and Motivation: Function and
        Mechanism" (*unpublished*)

1985   Alice Eagly (Purdue University)
        "Sex Differences in Social Behavior:
        A Social-Role Interpretation"

1986   Karl Pribram (Stanford University)
        "Brain Organization in Perception:
        Holonomy and Structure in Figural
        Processing" (*in press*)

1987   Abram Amsel (University of Texas at Austin)
        "Behaviorism, Neobehaviorism, and Cognitivism
        in Learning Theory: Historical and Contemporary Perspectives"

1989   Robert S. Siegler and Eric Jenkins
        (Carnegie-Mellon University)
        "How Children Discover New Strategies"

Eugene C. Lechelt, Coordinator
MacEachran Memorial Lecture Series

Sponsored by The Department of Psychology, The University of Alberta with the support of The Alberta Heritage Foundation for Medical Research in memory of John M. MacEachran, pioneer in Canadian psychology.

New honors come upon us,
Like strange garments,
Cleave not to our mold,
But with the aid of use
—Banquo in *MacBeth*

Strategy Discovery and Strategy Generalization

A child's mind is like a workshop. This workshop contains a remarkable collection of materials (knowledge) and tools (learning processes) that can be used to make new products (rules, strategies, hypotheses, schema, causal networks, etc). Some of the tools and materials are useful for a great many tasks. Many others are specialized for a particular purpose, but are invaluable when they are needed.

Orders constantly arrive at the workshop for products that need to be made. Most of the requested products are familiar, and the child already knows how to make them. Others are new, though. Choosing the tools and materials for building these new products can be frustrating, but it also challenges the workshop to produce its finest wares.

Many products that are fabricated in the process of meeting one order themselves become materials and tools for making additional products. For this reason, the broader the range of products the workshop has produced in the past, the greater its potential for meeting future demands. Realizing this potential, however, requires not only that diverse tools and materials be on hand but that they be efficiently organized. Otherwise, they will simply represent clutter.

The life of the workshop is not limited to its internal workings. It has daily contact with other workshops. These other workshops tend to be friendly, experienced, and eager to demonstrate new techniques. Still, there are limits to how helpful they can be. Often, they do not say how a particular job can be done. Even when they attempt to provide instructions, the ones they give are often confusing because they call for tools that the workshop has not yet acquired. Many of the greatest challenges must be met by discovering how to use available resources for novel purposes.

The workshop is a proud and industrious place. Its workers invent tools and materials even without outside requests for them. In part, this is due to knowing that the new discoveries may someday be useful. In part, it is due to a desire to find easier ways of getting jobs done. Not all of the efforts, however, can be attributed to foresight or laziness. Some are due to simple enjoyment of the work.

The purpose of this book is to explore how children's minds construct one of their most important products, new problem-solving strategies. The strategy-construction process is divided into two parts: strategy discovery and strategy generalization. Among the central issues that are addressed are the experiences that promote discovery and generalization of strategies, the qualities of children that predict who will make the discoveries and who will generalize them most widely, and how strategies differ from related cognitive activities such as procedures and plans.

THE ISSUE OF STRATEGY CONSTRUCTION

We accomplish most of our goals in unremarkable ways. Sometimes, however, we must abandon the routine. Highway repairs, forgotten wallets, malfunctioning slide projectors, lost keys, and many other minor tragedies challenge us daily. Often, we already know alternate approaches. Taking a different route to work, borrowing money for lunch, checking whether all of the proper connections have been made on the slide projector, and finding a janitor with a key provide straightforward ways around these momentary problems. Occasionally, however, we need to go beyond previously discovered or easily generated alternatives. That is, we need to construct a new strategy.

Although all of us must construct new strategies, the process may be especially prominent in the lives of children. As Brown and DeLoache (1978) noted, children are in a sense universal novices. They constantly need to discover strategies to cope with situations that adults find quite routine. They also need to find out where newly discovered strategies apply. Thus, they seem a particularly appropriate group for studying the process of strategy construction.

HISTORICAL BACKGROUND

The Role of Learning in Cognition

Construction of new strategies is one facet of the larger topic of learning. However, it is a facet that has historically received relatively little attention. The reasons for this are instructive.

Learning has been a central topic within psychology from the field's earliest days as a science. The grand theories of Thorndike, Guthrie, Skinner, and Hull established learning as *the* central topic in psychology in the 1930s, 1940s, and 1950s. However, construction of new strategies never became a major topic within these learning theories. Part of the reason was that the idea of "strategies" was uncommon; the standard unit of analysis was the stimulus–response connection. Another reason was that most of the tasks that were studied were extremely simple. To the extent that any strategy needed to be constructed, the strategy usually could be assembled very quickly.

The cognitive revolution of the late 1950s brought with it the strategy as a basic unit of analysis. This centrality was evident even in some of the earliest cognitive research: that of Newell and Simon (1956); Bruner, Goodnow, and Austin (1956); Brown, (1956); and Miller, Galanter, and Pribram (1960). Along with this attention to strategies and other higher order cognitive units, however, came a de-emphasis on learning. This de-emphasis represented an explicit decision concerning the approach that seemed most likely to advance rapidly understanding of cognition. As Newell and Simon (1972) commented:

> Turning to the performance-learning-development dimension, our emphasis on performance again represents a scientific bet. . . . The study of learning, if carried out with theoretical precision, must start with a model of a performing organism, so that one can represent, as learning, the changes in the model. . . . It is our judgment that in the present state of the art, the study of performance must be given precedence, even if the strategy is not costless. (pp. 7–8)

   This research approach did allow rapid progress in our understanding of strategies and other types of cognitive activity. However,
as Newell and Simon anticipated, it was not without cost. By the late
1970s, numerous investigators were lamenting the lack of data and the
paucity of cognitive theories of learning, especially complex, extra-
laboratory learning (e.g., Anderson, 1976; Bransford, 1979; Glaser,
1976; Stevenson, 1983; Voss, 1978). For example, Voss (1978) wrote,
"Although the concept of learning may be found in cognitive psychology, it also must be conceded that the cognitive view of learning is
vague, is abstract, and most important is lacking a substantive data
base" (p. 13). Similarly, Anderson (1976) commented, "Interest in the
mechanisms of procedural learning seems to have died in cognitive
psychology with the demise of the stimulus-response theories. . . . It
is important that cognitive psychology concern itself more with the
issue of learning, both because of its important practical implications
and because it serves to place important constraints on cognitive
theories" (p. 20).
   In the 1980s, research on learning of complex, extra-laboratory
skills assumed a more prominent place. Major theories of adult
cognition, such as those of Anderson (1983); Holland, Holyoak,
Nisbett, and Thagard (1986); McClelland and Rumelhart (1986); and
Newell (1989) have focused on problems of learning and induction. A
similar trend has been evident in cognitive–developmental theories,
such as those of Case (1985), Klahr (1984), Sternberg (1985), and
Siegler and Shrager (1984). There is considerable consensus now that
a model that does not account for knowledge acquisition is a seriously
incomplete model of cognition.
   Even with the resurgence of interest in learning, large gaps in our
understanding remain. One of the most serious of these involves our
lack of knowledge about how new strategies are constructed. A
number of current models deal quite well with the strengthening and
weakening of rules and strategies that already exist. However, this is
not sufficient. As Holland et al. (1986) noted, "Although it is possible
to understand much of learning in terms of revision of rule strength,
it is not possible to understand all of learning in that way. Somehow,
at some point, those rules that are to undergo strength revision have
to be generated" (p. 344).
   The generation of strategies over long and variable periods of time
is a special mystery. We usually think of learning as involving either a
gradual build up of associative strength of some behavior or as
involving the testing of hypotheses until one is found to be correct. It

is difficult to explain long-term strategy construction comfortably within either of these frameworks, however. If all that was needed for a strategy to appear was sufficient asociative strength, why would some novel strategies gain the required strength within 10 minutes, yet others require 10 weeks or months? If hypotheses were being tested, why would it often take so long for the new strategy to be hypothesized (or if the hypothesis were not in the set being sampled, how would it eventually get in there)?

Two barriers must be overcome for progress to be made in understanding this type of learning. One is an adequate empirical base. Because of the time and effort inherent to studying long-term strategy construction, few studies of the process have been conducted. The other barrier concerns ideas about mechanisms that could produce such discoveries. Conceiving of mechanisms that, like people, would form new strategies after not doing so on many previous occasions, is difficult. Yet we know from people's behavior that such mechanisms must exist.

Some Personal History

Any research program reflects the personal history that led the investigators to study the problem, and study it in a particular way, as well as the history of the field. For one of us (RS), studying the process of strategy construction represents a coming together of two main research programs pursued since the mid-1970s. The first project (the rule-assessment studies) focused on identifying *the* strategy a given child used to solve a set of problems, the sequence of strategies through which children's thinking progressed with age, and the ways in which existing rules and encodings influenced acquisition of new knowledge. The more recent project (the strategy-choice studies) has focused on identifying the diverse strategies that a given child uses to solve certain types of problems, the changes over time in the relative frequency of the strategies used by each child, and the mechanisms that enable children to choose adaptively among the multiple strategies they know and use for solving these problems.

The two sets of studies differ in numerous ways. The first group of studies examined children's performance on variants of Piaget's scientific reasoning tasks: balance scale, projection of shadows, and probability problems (Siegler, 1976, 1978); conservation of liquid quantity, solid quantity, and number problems (Siegler, 1981); time, speed, and distance problems (Siegler & Richards, 1979); and so on.

The latter group of studies focused on academic tasks such as addition, subtraction, and multiplication (Siegler, 1988a; Siegler & Shrager, 1984); spelling and reading (Siegler, 1986, 1988b); and time-telling (Siegler & McGilly, 1989). The first group emphasized the rule as the basic unit of analysis; the second group emphasized associations among strategies, problems, and answers. The earlier studies depicted development as a sharp qualitative change from use of one rule to use of another; the more recent ones depict development as a gradual change in the distribution of strategy use, with new strategies coexisting with, rather than replacing, previous ones.

In my own mind, at least, the two sets of studies form a natural progression. The initial studies focused on situations in which individual children consistently use a single rule (strategy). As I reflected on this property of the situations, I became increasingly convinced that although such situations are an interesting part of cognitive development, they are far from the whole story. Often, children (and adults) use a variety of strategies. Understanding both how they come to use a single consistent rule in some situations and how they come to use multiple approaches in others seemed important for understanding cognition in general. This was part of my motivation for focusing on problems on which children use multiple strategies rather than a single rule.

Another reason for moving from the one emphasis to the other concerned the complexity of the issues raised by the situations. At first glance, understanding children's problem-solving strategies on balance scale, projection of shadows, and conservation tasks sounds like it would be inherently more challenging than understanding how they solve arithmetic and time-telling problems. Intuitive estimates of the difficulty of understanding cognitive processes are often wildly misleading, however. The first computer simulations of cognitive activity (Newell & Simon, 1956) modeled quite well how people perform such high-level cognitive activities as solving logic problems. Other profound human accomplishments, such as playing chess, solving physics problems, and proving geometry theorems, quickly proved to be similarly tractable. Yet we remain unable to model such seemingly mundane activities as seeing, hearing, and understanding language. In the same way, understanding how children choose among multiple strategies on such "simple" tasks as adding and subtracting small numbers has proven to be more challenging than understanding their use of a single strategy on scientific reasoning and other "high-level" tasks. Thus, although it may sound ironic, part of the reason that I moved from studying balance scales, projection of shadows, and conservation to studying addition and subtraction was that understanding the issues raised by the latter posed the greater challenge for me.[1]

One difference between the earlier and later projects was critical to the present investigation. Although both sets of studies have focused on learning processes, the nature of the processes differs. The learning processes of central interest in the earlier studies involved acquisition of new problem-solving strategies. Those in the later studies involved changing frequencies of use of existing strategies.

The experiments that are reported in this book represent a synthesis of the two types of change processes. Like the earlier studies, they focus on acquisition of new strategies. Like the more recent studies, they focus on situations in which any given strategy, new or old, will be only one among several approaches that children know and use. In such situations, new strategies do not replace previous ones (at least not for a long time), but rather find a niche among them. This means that the research in this monograph is aimed at explaining not only how new strategies are first generated but also how they find their niches among previously acquired approaches.

Two particular themes that emerged in the earlier studies of learning also emerged as important in the present ones. One was the influence of existing knowledge on learning. New strategies do not emerge in a vacuum. Instead, they seem to be constructed from the materials of previous strategies. At least in this domain, the strategy-construction process seems to involve combining parts of existing strategies in novel ways, or grafting on new segments to existing procedures, rather than creating the new strategy out of whole cloth.

The second common theme was the importance of encoding in strategy construction. In the earlier studies, young children often failed to learn from relevant experience on balance scale and temporal duration problems because they did not encode relevant dimensions such as the distance of the weights on each side from the fulcrum (Siegler, 1976, 1983). In the present study, much of the challenge of constructing new strategies appears to lie in encoding which goals were

---

[1]At least for the present. The issues raised by a given type of cognitive activity change with progress in a field. It is not tasks that are simple or complex, but rather the types of issues that can be raised about cognitive activities on them. Thus, at one time, a desire to pursue more complex phenomena might lead to a switch from studying Task A to studying Task B; at a later time, the same desire to study more complex phenomena might motivate a change back to studying Task A.

met by different parts of existing strategies and in selecting the right segments of existing strategies for inclusion in the new strategy.

Methods for Studying Learning

Studying complex extra-laboratory learning poses not only conceptual difficulties but also methodological ones. At least three distinct research strategies have been developed for dealing with these methodological challenges. Each approach has distinct strengths and weaknesses. However, one of them, the microgenetic approach, seems particularly well suited for studying the construction of strategies over long periods of time. Here, we review the three methods for investigating complex learning and discuss why we concluded that the microgenetic approach was best suited for the goals of the present investigation.

One approach to studying learning of complex real-world skills has been to focus on quantitative changes in performance with practice (Fitts & Posner, 1967; Mazur & Hastie, 1978). Here, individuals are followed over a very large number of trials as they became increasingly competent at executing a skill. Often, the emphasis is on the shape of the mathematical function that best describes the reduction in solution times with practice. Newell and Rosenbloom (1981) summarized much of this literature in their article on the ubiquity of the power law as a description of practice effects in such diverse areas as reading inverted letters, solving geometric proof problems, rolling cigars, and learning text-editing commands. This approach has yielded striking quantitative regularities in the rate of improvement of performance with practice. By its focus on purely quantitative measures, however, the approach precludes obtaining qualitative information about knowledge and processes underlying construction of new strategies. Thus, it is not well suited to the issues of central interest in the present investigation (though see Rosenbloom & Newell, 1986, for ways in which a rich theoretical framework can be used to explain how such quantitative regularities can arise.

A second strategy for studying learning of complex, real-world skills has been to examine how students learn from explicit instruction. Such studies typically include identification of a concept or skill that students have difficulty acquiring, analysis of why the learners' current capabilities or the usual instruction make the new understanding difficult to obtain, and formulation of a new type of instruction that will overcome the difficulty. Experiments test whether the new instruction is effective in producing the hoped-for progress. Not surprisingly, this approach has been particularly prominent in educational areas such as reading (Bradley & Bryant, 1983; Palincsar & Brown, 1984), writing (Bereiter & Scardamalia, 1987; Gray, 1977), mathematics (Case, 1985; Schoenfeld, 1987), and computer programming (Klahr & Carver, 1988). It has proven useful both theoretically and practically; much learning is in response to instruction, and what is learned from instruction often differs from what the teacher intended. Because teaching is such a complex activity, however, it often is impossible to identify the point at which a given child acquired a new strategy or the specific factors of the teaching strategy that led to the discovery. Again, the approach does not seem ideal for studying strategy construction.

A third approach to learning of complex real-world knowledge and skills, the *microgenetic approach,* combines a number of advantages of the other approaches. The term *microgenetic approach* has been used in different ways by different investigators (e.g., Kuhn & Phelps, 1982; Metz, 1985; Paris, Newman, & McVey, 1982). In our view, microgenetic methods have two key properties: (a) Subjects are observed over an extended period of time; (b) Their learning is subjected to intensive trial-by-trial analysis, with the goal being to infer the underlying representations and processes that gave rise to both qualitative and quantitative aspects of learning.

Most studies that we would label *microgenetic* have involved 10 to 50 sessions and 10 to 50 hours of experience, although one heroic research program involved 250 to 1,000 sessions and 200 to 800 hours of experience (Chase & Ericsson, 1981; Ericsson, Chase & Faloon, 1980; Staszewski, 1987, 1988). Because of the time and effort required to conduct such studies, there have not been many. For the same reason, most of those that have been done are single-subject studies. Among these are Anderson, Greeno, Kline, and Neves' (1981) study of acquisition of geometry knowledge, Lawler's (1985) study of acquisition of understanding of LOGO, Staszewski's (1988) study of acquisition of mental multiplication skills, and Chase and Ericsson's (1981) and Staszewski's (1987) studies of superior digit memory. A few microgenetic studies have examined larger numbers of subjects (10–20). Three of these are Kuhn and Phelps' (1982) study of discovery of scientific reasoning strategies, Metz' (1985) study of acquisition of strategies for solving problems involving gears, and Schauble's (1989) study of induction of the causal structure of a microworld. In all of these studies, investigators intensely scrutinized each subject's performance, with the goal of inferring how skills, knowledge, and understanding change with experience.

The microgenetic approach has a number of advantages for studying strategy discovery. It allows identification of the exact point at which a new strategy was first used. This identification of when the strategy was first adopted allows examination of the circumstances leading up to the discovery and of the process of generalization once the strategy was discovered. It also makes possible identification of short-lived strategies that, despite their fleeting use, may play critical bridging roles in the acquisition of more stable strategies (Flavell & Wohlwill, 1969).

The type of observations that the microgenetic approach can yield are clearly illustrated in Kuhn and Phelps' (1982) study of the development of scientific reasoning strategies. They presented 15 fourth and fifth graders with chemical interactions problems similar to those used by Inhelder and Piaget (1958). On these problems, children needed to discover the role played by each of several chemicals in determining whether a solution changed color. Kuhn and Phelps found that even after children first used the most efficient experimental strategy available, they continued to use a variety of unsystematic strategies as well. This was true of literally every subject in their study. They also found that only a few children's first use of a strategy was accomplished through a sudden conscious burst of insight. For the others, the discovery process was less conscious and often less explicit. Beyond this, they found that even children who had earlier seemed to abandon the less systematic strategies returned to them when confronted with slightly more difficult problems. These phenomena seem critical to the process of strategy construction. They also seem to be much more likely to be identified through use of a microgenetic approach than through other methods.

As with any research strategy, microgenetic methods entail certain disadvantages. Observing individual children's performance over very large numbers of trials, and analyzing the performance on a trial-by-trial basis, is inherently expensive. This is even more the case when concurrent or immediately retrospective verbal protocols are obtained on each trial, as they often are in microgenetic studies. The usual compromise with reality is to limit sample sizes to one or a few subjects. However, such small sample sizes, together with the fact that different children generate strategies at different times and in the context of different problems, prevent the use of standard inferential statistical methods for many comparisons of interest.

Another, somewhat paradoxical, problem generated by microgenetic methods is that they make investigators extremely aware of the distance between the general conclusions that can be drawn and the complexities of each subject's performance. When the available data are limited to "hard" measures, such as solution times or percent correct on each problem, a single simple model often can account for most of the variance in the data. This creates a warm feeling within the experimenter, a sense that we are really beginning to understand cognition. When the data include subjects' explanations of how they solved each of hundreds or thousands of problems, however, the idiosyncracies of individual performance emerge more clearly and become much harder to ignore. Both the inclusion of self-reports as data and the examination of individual subjects' performance over large numbers of trials contribute to this awareness of variation within and between individuals. Using microgenetic methods can be humbling, because they make evident the discrepancy between the richness of cognitive activity and our limited understanding of it.

Nonetheless, for purposes of studying strategy construction, the microgenetic approach seems to be the method of choice. It reveals key aspects of the acquisition process that would remain unknown if other methods were used.

AN A PRIORI ANALYSIS OF STRATEGY CONSTRUCTION

What is a Strategy?

To understand the process of strategy construction requires clarity about the nature of the strategies that are being constructed. We define a *strategy* as any procedure that is nonobligatory and goal directed. The nonobligatory feature is included to distinguish strategies from procedures in general. Procedures, unlike strategies, may represent the only way to achieve a goal. For example, pulling back the gearshift on a car to move from first gear to second is a procedure but not a strategy, because there is no alternative way to shift.

We define strategies as goal directed to distinguish them from activities that either are not intended to accomplish goals or that accomplish goals other than the ones intended. Drawing a picture can be a strategy for amusing oneself, for making money, for impressing a friend, or for expressing an emotion. However, any particular act of drawing is only a strategy with regard to the goals it is intended to accomplish.

Our definition explicitly does not stipulate that a strategy must be consciously formulated or the product of a conscious or rational choice. Viewing strategies in this way differentiates them from plans, which are usually conceived as inherently involving consciousness. This emphasis on consciousness is evident in Scholnick and Friedman's (1987) definition of a plan as "behavior that is voluntary, self-conscious, and intended" (p. 5). It seems useful to have one term, *strategies,* that encompasses activities in which choice processes can be either conscious or unconscious, and another term, *plans,* that refers only to consciously adopted strategies. Thus, we define strategies as differing from procedures in that strategies necessarily involve choice, and as differing from plans in that the choice process is not necessarily conscious.

Strategies are sometimes viewed as relatively grand entities that encompass a variety of means toward an end. This conception is embodied in the military distinction between strategies and tactics, and in the organization theory concept of strategic planning. Bisanz and LeFevre (in press) suggested that such an approach might also be applied to cognition. In particular, they argued that the entire Siegler and Shrager (1984) strategy-choice model should be viewed as a strategy, and particular activities within it, such as counting fingers, should be viewed as procedures within the strategy. The Bisanz and LeFevre approach seems reasonable in most respects, but has one important disadvantage. This involves the issue of choice. Adopting a strategy implies that another strategy might have been adopted. The use of strategies in military and commercial contexts reflects this property; a commander or chief executive officer adopts one of several approaches that might be chosen. Within the Siegler and Shrager model, however, people have no alternative but to behave in accord with the strategy-choice mechanism, because it is hypothesized to be a basic part of the human cognitive architecture. Alternative strategies, such as counting fingers and decomposing a problem into two simpler ones, vary across individuals and are chosen among, but the strategy-choice mechanism itself is invariant. Thus, given the centrality of choice to the meaning of strategies, it seems best to reserve the term *strategies* for procedures that are chosen among.

One consequence of the present view of strategies is that retrieval qualifies as a strategy, as long as it is directed at a goal and is used in a context in which other strategies can meet the same goal. Although this implication may be nonintuitive, we view it as one source of evidence for the usefulness of the present definition. Frequency of use of retrieval responds to the same influences that affect use of other, more prototypic strategies. For example, retrieval, like other strategies is used most often on problems where it produces the greatest accuracy and speed relative to alternative approaches (Siegler, 1987a, in press). Similarly, early in the learning process, use of retrieval to solve a given problem, like use of other strategies, varies from trial to trial. Successful retrieval of an answer to a problem one day often gives way to use of a different strategy to solve the same problem the next day (Siegler, 1987b; Siegler & McGilly, 1989). Further, contemporary analyses, which emphasize spreading activation and parallel distributed processing, indicate that retrieval is not a simple unitary act. Instead, like other strategies, it is itself the product of complex cognitive activity. Thus, it seems useful to think of retrieval as a kind of strategy whenever it is one among several procedures that can be used to attain a goal.

Assumptions About Existing Knowledge

Any analysis of strategy construction critically depends on assumptions about existing knowledge. We make three main assumptions here. The first is that in many cases, new strategies will enter territories that are already inhabited. People possess or can readily generate multiple strategies for performing almost any task that they encounter. The strategies are not always ideal, but they are generally reasonable. For example, if a person forgot a key, he or she could go to a janitor or a co-worker, try a credit card, drive home, call a wife or husband if they had a copy of the key, and so on. Recent studies have found that individual subjects use multiple strategies on tasks as diverse as question answering (Reder, 1987); referential communication (Kahan & Richards, 1986); number series problems (LeFevre & Bisanz, 1986); language acquisition (Maratsos, 1983); decision making (Payne, Bettman, & Johnson, 1988); drawing causal inferences (Shultz, Fisher, Pratt, & Rulf, 1986); and solving arithmetic, spelling, reading, and time-telling problems (Geary & Burlingham-DuBree, 1989; Goldman, Pellegrino, & Mertz, 1988; Siegler, 1986, 1988b; Siegler & McGilly, 1989). Thus, when a new strategy is constructed, it often will need to compete against alternative methods for performing the task.

The second assumption about the cognitive environments into

which newly constructed strategies enter is that each strategy is used most often on problems where its advantages relative to other strategies are greatest. The strongest evidence for this assumption comes from studies of 5- to 9-year-olds' addition and subtraction (Geary & Burlingham-DuBree, 1989; Siegler, 1987a, 1987b). Even preschoolers generally use each strategy most often on problems where that approach yields fast and accurate performance relative to the performance that other strategies produce. For example, retrieval, the fastest way in which to generate answers to addition and subtraction problems, is used wherever it will yield accurate performance. Counting up from the larger addend (e. g., solving 2 + 6 by thinking "6, 7, 8") is used most often on problems such as 9 + 2, where the smaller addend is small (thus making the strategy easy to execute) and where the difference between the addends is large (thus making the strategy especially advantageous relative to alternative strategies, such as counting from one). Counting from 1 is used most often on problems such as 9 + 8, where both retrieval and counting up from the larger addend are difficult to execute correctly. Thus, at least strategies that have been known for a reasonably long time appear to be used most often in the circumstances where they are most useful. By obtaining longitudinal data in which the first uses of a strategy were included, we could investigate whether this is also true when strategies are first discovered.

The third assumption is that knowledge about where the strategies should be used comes primarily from past outcomes produced by the strategies rather than through a rational metacognitive analysis of where the strategies should be most useful. If children needed to base their strategy choices on logical analyses of each strategy's strengths and weaknesses, it is doubtful that they would ever be able to choose as wisely as they do. However, through repeated use of different strategies, children learn about the overall speed and accuracy yielded by each strategy, the effort required to use it, and the types of problems on which it is most effective. Even students near the bottom of their class in standardized achievement test scores choose strategies adaptively in domains where they have experience, such as addition, subtraction, and word identification (Siegler, 1988b). How experience with strategies helps subsequent strategy selection can be illustrated by contrasting people's slow and frequently unfortunate choices of strategies on unfamiliar tasks with their fast, confident, and seemingly effortless choices on familiar ones. (Contrast the selection of tools and materials of an experienced mechanic with that of the typical car owner.)

Assumptions About Construction of New Strategies

The process of strategy construction takes place over time. Sometimes the process takes only a few seconds or minutes, but for many of the most interesting strategies, it takes weeks, months, or even years. Time provides an important constraint on the ways in which strategy construction could occur. Even cursory consideration of it indicates serious flaws in current simulations of how people make discoveries. Some models, such as Langley, Zytkow, Simon, and Bradshaw's (1986) BACON model learn in a single trial rules that it took scientists many years to learn. For these models, the problem is why do people take so long to discover new strategies. Other models, such as McClelland's (1988) model of balance scale learning, take hundreds of trials to generate behavior that children generate in less than one-tenth the time. For these models, the problem is how people discover new strategies as quickly as they do.

Considering the process of strategy construction along a dimension of time suggests a basic division of the process into two periods: an initial period of *strategy discovery* and a later period of *strategy generalization*. The strategy discovery period involves the time leading up to and including the first use of the new procedure. The strategy generalization period involves the transition from having used the strategy once to using it in the full range of situations where it is the most effective approach.

The discovery period may appear to be both the more essential and the more interesting of the two. Our everyday prototype of strategy discovery seems to be Archimedes' insight in the bathtub concerning how to find out whether the king's crown was made from pure gold. Within this prototype, strategy discovery involves a sudden burst of understanding and is accompanied by a conscious "aha" (or "Eureka") experience; the discoverer not only uses the strategy for the first time but immediately understands why it works and what types of problems it can solve. The appeal of this view lies not only in its drama but also in its simplicity. Discovery is seen as involving a sudden, discontinuous change from not knowing to knowing.

In contrast, there is no prototype of generalization that seems comparably interesting. History does not record the range of problems that Archimedes became able to solve through reference to the densities of component materials. Relative to discovery of new strategies, generalization of existing strategies often seems gradual, incremental, automatic, and rather dull.

Research findings give reason to question the validity of these stereotypes, however. Studies of problem solving have shown repeatedly that college students who have discovered a strategy in one context often do not spontaneously extend the strategy to formally identical but superficially dissimilar contexts (e.g., Reed, Ernst, & Banerji; 1974 Simon & Hayes, 1976;). Those interested in education have long lamented the problem of inert knowledge (e.g., Bransford & Stein, 1984), where children fail to apply strategies they know to new problems (Chipman, Segal, & Glaser, 1985; National Assessment of Educational Progress, 1983). As Kail (1984) commented, "It is one thing to use a learning strategy successfully once; it is quite another for students to use the trained strategy thereafter on new tasks" (p. 31).

The difficulty here is not that people are stupid, but rather is inherent to the process of generalization. Consider Johnson-Laird's (1983) wobbly table problem. How would you fix a wobbly four-legged table? Wedging something under the shorter leg or legs is a strategy that most people generate. What if it was a three-legged table? Many people generate the same solution. But generalization of the strategy to this seemingly analogous problem is inappropriate; three-legged tables cannot wobble. As this example illustrates, people often only comprehend the nature of a strategy when they have gained experience with problems where the strategy does and does not apply. Learning the conditions of applicability of a strategy may often pose at least as large a challenge as discovering the strategy in the first place.

The contrast between strategy discovery as representing sudden, discontinuous breakthroughs and strategy generalization as representing gradual, incremental changes also may be more illusory than real. The qualitative behavioral change from never having used a strategy to using it for the first time may be the product of underlying quantitative changes in representations and processes. Some recent computer simulations of strategy change (e.g., McClelland & Jenkins, in press) posit that even the first use of a strategy is due to a gradually changing pattern of connection strengths rather than to any qualitative novelty in representations or processes. Biographies of gifted scientific discoverers such as Darwin also show that what seem in retrospect to be dramatic qualitative breakthroughs are in fact the culmination of a long series of smaller realizations concerning how existing ideas can be recombined (Gruber, 1981). Such biographies reveal that it often is difficult to establish exactly what constitutes a new discovery and what constitutes a coalescence of existing ideas or a generalization of an already-known strategy to a new situation. An innovation may constitute a new discovery if considered within the context of a particular domain but may be seen as a generalization of another approach if considered within a wider context.

On the other side of the equation, the strategy generalization process can involve sudden, seemingly discontinuous changes. Studies of analogical problem solving (e.g., Gentner & Toupin, 1986; Holland et al., 1986) document how generalization of strategies to new contexts can occur through sudden insights into the nature of the strategy and the problems. Seen from this perspective, the first use of a strategy in a domain is an important milestone, but by no means the end of the strategy construction process. Both the strategy-discovery and the strategy-generalization phases represent a mix of qualitative and quantitative changes. In important senses, a person has not fully constructed a strategy until the person extends it to the entire range of situations in which it is useful.

SOME ISSUES CONCERNING STRATEGY CONSTRUCTION

What Experiences Promote Strategy Construction?

Most psychological models of how rules and strategies are learned have portrayed learning as a reaction to failure. For example, traditional models of concept formation (e.g., Levine, 1966) indicated that people switch hypotheses when they receive feedback that the current hypothesis is incorrect. Piagetian theory portrayed acquisition of new schemas as arising out of cognitive conflict, provoked by the inability of existing structures to assimilate new experiences. Information-processing approaches (e.g., Siegler, 1983) depicted new rules as being formed when existing rules are unable to correctly predict the outcomes of problems.

Although failure is unquestionably one motive for learning, it is not the only one. People often learn new strategies even when existing ones produce consistently correct performance. Markman (1978) found that 8-year-olds solve class inclusion problems through a counting procedure, whereas 11-year-olds solve the problems through logical deduction. Siegler (1981) found that 5-year-olds solve number conservation problems through counting and pairing, whereas 8-year-olds solve the problems on the basis of the type of transformation that was performed. Groen and Resnick (1977) found that children who are just learning to add, solve problems by counting from 1, whereas children who have had a large amount of practice solve them by counting from the larger number. In all cases, correct execution of the old as well as the new procedure would produce entirely correct performance. Failure of existing approaches probably increases motivation to learn *now,* but does not seem necessary for learning to occur. Cognitive efficiency, aesthetic elegance, and novelty are other values that may motivate strategy discoveries.

One goal of the present book was to determine what, in addition to failure to solve problems, leads to construction of new strategies. The examples just given suggest that children sometimes formulate new strategies whose advantage is that they can be executed faster and with less effort than existing ones. Whether children anticipate that such strategies will be more efficient, and which experiences lead them to form such strategies, are unknown. Appealing to insights or understanding of the problem leaves open the question of why such discoveries require such a long time. The challenge is to understand simultaneously how children can construct such strategies at all and why it often takes them so long to do so.

Who Will Discover a Strategy?

Three major approaches to the problem of predicting who will learn have been to emphasize intelligence, knowledge, and age. The link between learning and intelligence goes back at least to Binet (1890), who developed his IQ test to predict which students could not learn well enough to benefit from typical classroom instruction. The belief in a link between intelligence and learning also was evident in the definitions of intelligence offered in a famous 1921 symposium on the nature of intelligence. Among these definitions of intelligence were "the ability to learn" (Buckingham, 1921), the capacity to learn (Dearborn, 1921), and "the capacity to acquire capacity" (Woodrow, 1921). In keeping with this view, clear empirical differences between children of above-average and average IQs and between children of average and below-average IQs have emerged in rate of learning new strategies and degree of generalization of the strategies to new problems (Campione, Brown, & Bryant, 1985). Similar differences have emerged between people of high and low knowledge within a particular domain. The view that content knowledge is important in discovery of new strategies goes back at least as far as Thorndike's (1903) identical elements theory. In a classic experiment, Thorndike demonstrated that possessing relevant knowledge aided kittens trying to escape from boxes. Gagne (1968) developed in greater detail ideas about how prior knowledge aided discovery of new strategies in more complex domains, particularly mathematics. Chi's (1978) demonstration that knowledge of chess enabled children more readily to formulate efficient strategies for solving the knight's tour problem continued this tradition.

The idea that age and learning are related is inherent to such classical constructs as readiness, critical periods, and the problem of the match. For example, Huey (1908) commented that "much that is now strenuously struggled for and methodized over in these early years of reading will come of themselves with growth, and when the child's sense organs and nervous system are stronger. . . . Reading will be learned fast when the time comes" (pp. 303, 309). Older children have proved more able than younger ones to discover strategies for remembering, reasoning, solving numerous types of problems, and transferring the strategies to new tasks (e. g., Inhelder, Sinclair, & Bovet, 1974; O'Sullivan & Pressley, 1984; Siegler, 1976).

Microgenetic methods of the type used in the present study have some unique advantages for determining predictors of learning. Because they involve ongoing observation of children, they allow identification of factors that immediately precede strategy discovery (e.g., reaching a certain mental or chronological age, attaining a particular type of knowledge, having an insight), and also identification of "leading indicators" that enable us to predict well in advance which children are most likely to make the discoveries. Additionally, because they allow identification of when a strategy is first used, they enable the investigator to separate the length of time required to discover the strategy from its subsequent frequency of use. Different factors might govern these two outcomes. For example, a child who already knew a lot about a domain might both discover a strategy more quickly than other children (through analogies to existing strategies) and subsequently use it less (because some of the existing strategies were more effective than the newly discovered one). Finally, because the microgenetic approach involves intensive study of each child, it enables us to go beyond the truism that "children who know more learn more" to identify the particular aspects of knowledge in a domain that are related to strategy discovery and generalization.

2

Strategy Choices and the Development of Arithmetic Skills

In the last chapter, we listed three assumptions about the contexts into which newly discovered strategies typically enter: that people already know one or more strategies for solving problems in them; that people use each strategy most frequently on the problems where its advantages relative to other strategies are greatest; and that using the strategies produces knowledge about where the strategies should be used in the future. These assumptions may not sound particularly radical, but taking them seriously leads to models fundamentally different than those traditionally proposed to account for cognition and cognitive development.

Children's arithmetic has proven to be a particularly advantageous area in which to study strategy choices. Children use a variety of strategies to solve arithmetic problems. The strategies are quite discrete from each other, which simplifies the task of assessing strategy use. The unique precision of numbers, together with the nature of the strategies, yields straightforward predictions concerning the patterns of data that should emerge if a given strategy is being used. This allows rigorous tests of alternative models. Learning includes both qualitative and quantitative changes in knowledge and performance. Finally, arithmetic is of considerable practical importance; it is used on an everyday basis by both children and adults, it provides a foundation for more advanced mathematical skills such as algebra, and it is the focus of most mathematics instruction for several years of elementary school.

These characteristics also made arithmetic an appealing area in which to study strategy construction. Further adding to its attractiveness for this purpose was our relatively good understanding of other aspects of performance and development in the domain. Understanding the strategies that are already being used in a domain is essential for understanding a number of aspects of strategy construction: the motivation for constructing a new strategy, the niche that the new strategy will fill among the existing ones, and the components of existing strategies that are available for constructing the new approach. Thus, the fact that children's existing strategies for solving arithmetic problems were relatively well understood paved the way for exploring how they construct new strategies for solving such problems.

This chapter summarizes current knowledge of children's strategies for solving simple arithmetic problems. First, we examine evidence that individual children know and use multiple arithmetic strategies and that a combination of immediately retrospective verbal reports and video recordings of ongoing performance can yield accurate assessments of which strategy was used on each trial. Then, we describe evidence concerning the conditions under which children use each strategy. Next, we describe a detailed model of how children choose among the strategies and how their choices change over the course of development. Finally, we examine what is known about how children discover new arithmetic strategies. Most of the examples are from young children's single-digit addition, because this is the context in which the strategy-construction research described in this volume was conducted. Similar examples can be found for subtraction in Siegler (1987a), for multiplication in Siegler (1988b), for spelling in Siegler (1986), for serial recall in McGilly and Siegler (1989), and for time telling in Siegler and McGilly (1989).

EVIDENCE THAT CHILDREN
USE DIVERSE STRATEGIES

Until recently, cognitive models depicted children of a given age as consistently using a single addition strategy. The most prominent of these models was Groen and Parkman's (1972) min model. Groen and Parkman observed that the size of the smaller addend was an excellent predictor of first graders' solution times on simple addition problems. This led them to postulate that children of this age consistently use the *min strategy* to solve such problems. The min strategy involves counting up from the larger addend the number of times indicated by the smaller addend. For example, a child using the min strategy to solve "3 + 6" would start at 6 and count upward 3 counts (the child would think "6, 7, 8, 9"). Groen and Parkman hypothesized that the only source of variation in solution times for different problems was the number of counts upward from the larger addend that were needed to solve the problem. Thus, 3 + 6, 6 + 3, and 4 + 3 would all produce the same solution times, because all required 3 upward counts; 2 + 3, 3 + 2, and 2 + 9 all would require one fewer count, and therefore one unit less time. Within the min model, then, young children's solution times are a linear function of the smaller addend because such children always add by counting from the larger addend, and the greater the size of the smaller addend, the more counts (and the more time) required to reach the sum.

A variety of findings, primarily based on chronometric data, supported the view that young children consistently add in the way postulated by the min model. The size of the smaller addend has consistently been the best predictor of first and second graders' solution times (Ashcraft, 1982, 1987; Kaye, Post, Hall, & Dineen, 1986; Svenson, 1975). It has proved to be a good predictor in absolute as well as relative terms, accounting for 60% to 75% of the variance in solution times in a number of studies. These studies have included children in special classes for poor students as well as children in standard classes, and children in Europe as well as in North America (Svenson & Broquist, 1975). The model fits individual children's solution times as well as group averages (Groen & Resnick, 1977; Kaye et al., 1986; Svenson, 1975).

The one discordant note came from mathematics educators' reports of what children said they did when they solved arithmetic problems (e.g., Baroody, 1984; Carpenter & Moser, 1982; Fuson, 1982). The children reported using a variety of strategies. Often an individual child would be classified as using five or more approaches.

Thus, the conclusions derived from chronometric data and from verbal reports conflicted. One possibility was that children's verbal reports were inaccurate. Even adults' verbal reports are often suspect (Nisbett & Wilson, 1977); young children may be even less accurate than adults in describing their cognitive processes (Brainerd, 1973). Another possibility, however, was that the verbal reports were accurate and the chronometric analyses misleading. In particular, different variability of solution times generated by different strategies and intercorrelations among independent and dependent variables might lead to a data pattern consistent with use of a single strategy when in fact multiple strategies were being used (for statistical arguments showing how this could occur in the specific case of addition, see Siegler, 1987b).

To determine whether 5- to 7-year-olds consistently use the min strategy or use a variety of strategies, Siegler (1987b) presented kindergarteners, first graders, and second graders with 45 addition problems. On these problems, the larger addend ranged from 4 to 17, the smaller addend from 1 to 10, and the sum from 5 to 23. Initially, problems were presented in the form, "If you had N oranges and I gave you M more, how many would you have then?" As children became familiar with the task, the question was simplified to "What is M + N?" Both solution time and verbal report data were collected for each child's performance on each trial.

The overall pattern of results replicated those of both the chronometric and the verbal report studies. Solution times for each problem were a linear function of the size of the smaller addend; smaller addend size accounted for 76% of the variance in median times on each problem. If these analyses were the only ones conducted, the usual conclusion would have been reached, namely that first and second graders consistently use the min strategy to add.

Also as in previous studies, the children's verbal reports suggested a quite different picture. The min strategy was but one of five approaches that they reported using (Table 2.1). They also said that they counted from 1, decomposed difficult problems into easier ones [for example 12 + 3 = 10 + (2 + 3)], retrieved answers, and guessed.

TABLE 2.1
Percentage of Use of Each Strategy by Children of Each Age (from Siegler, 1987b)

Grade			Strategy		Guess or
	Retrieval	Min	Decomposition	Count-all	No Response
Kindergarten	16	30	2	22	30
Grade 1	44	38	9	1	8
Grade 2	45	40	11	0	5
Overall	35	36	7	8	14

This reporting of diverse strategies characterized individual as well as group performance; most children reported using at least three approaches. Not only did children not report using the min strategy on every trial, they only said they had used it on 36% of trials. At no age did they report using it on more than 40% of trials.

Thus, the question remained: Were children consistently using the min strategy to add, or were they using multiple strategies? The decisive data came from dividing solution times and errors on each problem according to the strategy the child was classified as using on the trial. If the chronometric data were valid and the verbal reports misleading, then the min model would be expected to account for solution times on each problem regardless of which strategy children reported using. On the other hand, if the verbal reports data were valid and the chronometric analyses misleading, the min model would be expected to fit solution times when children said they used the min strategy, but not when they said they used other approaches.

The data were clear. On trials where children reported using the min strategy, the min model was an even better predictor of solution times on each problem than in past studies or in the present data set as a whole. It accounted for 86% of the variance in solution times (Table 2.2). In contrast, on trials where they reported using one of the other strategies, the min model was never a good predictor of performance, either in absolute terms or relative to other predictors. It never accounted for as much as 40% of the variance, was never either the best or the second best predictor of the times, and never added significant independent variance to that which could be accounted for by other predictors.

Similar findings emerged on the measure of percent errors on each problem. When children were classified as using the min strategy, the size of the smaller addend was the best predictor of their percentage of errors on each problem. It accounted for 74% of the variance in percent errors on each problem. However, when they said they used one of the other strategies, the size of the smaller addend was never either the best or the second best predictor, never accounted for more than 40% of the variance in percent errors, and never contributed significant independent variance. These and a variety of other data converged in indicating that children used the strategies that they reported using and that they employed them on those trials where they said they had.

The finding that children use multiple addition strategies has been replicated by other laboratories studying preschoolers (Geary &

TABLE 2.2
Best Predictor of Median Solution Time and Percent Errors on Each Problem (from Siegler, 1987b)

Strategy	Best Predictor	R^2
A. Solution Times		
All trials	Smaller addend	76
Retrieval	Sum	30
Min	Smaller addend	86
Decomposition	Sum squared	42
Count-all	Sum	35
Guessing	No significant predictors	
B. Errors		
All trials	Smaller addend	78
Retrieval	Sum squared	30
Min	Smaller addend	74
Decomposition	Sum squared	64
Count-all	Sum	35
Guessing	No significant predictors	

Burlingham-DuBree, 1989), third and fourth graders (Goldman, Mertz, & Pellegrino, in press), and children with learning disabilities (Goldman et al., 1988). Both self-reports and videotaped records of overt behavior indicate that even 4-year-olds, children of the age studied in the experiments reported in this volume, use multiple strategies. They sometimes put up fingers and count them, sometimes retrieve answers from memory, sometimes put up fingers and then answer without counting, and sometimes count without obvious external referents. Again, this is not a case of one child using one strategy and another child a different one. Rather, the majority of preschoolers have been found to use at least three addition strategies (Siegler & Robinson, 1982). Even the same problem presented to the same child on two consecutive days frequently leads to one strategy on one day and a different strategy on the next day (Siegler, 1987a).

Recognizing that individual children use multiple strategies leads to changes in our views of the acquisition process as well as in our views of performance at any one time. Traditionally, development of arithmetic (and many other skills and concepts) has been depicted as a progression through a sequence of strategies. These strategies have been viewed as having a 1:1 relation to age; children of one age were said to use one strategy, and children of another age a different one.

For example, Ashcraft (1982) found that the best predictor of solution times of first and second graders was the size of the smaller addend, that the best predictor of the solution times of fourth graders, older children, and adults was the size of the squared sum, and that the two variables predicted third graders' solution times equally well. Based on these data, he concluded that the first and second graders consistently used the min strategy, that the older children and adults consistently used retrieval, and that some third graders used one approach and some the other.

Recognizing that children of any one age use diverse strategies, however, leads to the realization that this progression is much too simple. Development involves changes in the mix of existing strategies as well as construction of new ones and abandonment of old ones. The data of Siegler and Shrager (1984), Siegler (1987a), Goldman et al. (1988), and Geary and Burlingham-Dubree (1989) indicate that different addition strategies undergo a variety of developmental courses during early childhood. Frequency of the sum strategy (e.g., solving 2 + 3 by counting "1, 2 . . . 1, 2, 3 . . . 1, 2, 3, 4, 5") steadily declines, frequency of retrieval steadily increases, and frequency of decomposition and of the min strategy increases and then declines.

These data suggest three main conclusions. First, at any one time, individual children use diverse strategies to solve arithmetic problems. Second, changes over time include changes in the mix of strategies as well as introduction of new strategies. Third, children's strategies for solving arithmetic problems can be assessed on a trial-by-trial basis by obtaining immediately retrospective verbal reports and videorecordings of ongoing problem-solving activities.

THE VALUE OF USING DIVERSE STRATEGIES

Children derive substantial advantages from using multiple approaches. This can be seen especially clearly in their choices of whether to state a retrieved answer or to use a *back-up strategy*. A back-up strategy is defined as any strategy other than retrieval; thus, probability of back-up strategy use is always 1 minus probability of retrieval. Examples of back-up strategies include counting from 1 or from the larger addend to add, adding one multiplicand the number of times indicated by the other to multiply, sounding out the letters in a word to read, and looking up a word in the dictionary to spell.

Both retrieval and back-up strategies have clear, although different, advantages. Retrieval can be executed much faster. Back-up strategies can yield accurate performance on problems where retrieval cannot. Ideally, children would use retrieval most often on problems where that fast approach could be executed accurately and would use backup strategies most often where they were necessary for accurate performance.

In all of the domains we have studied, children's strategy choices have followed exactly this pattern. On easy problems, children rely primarily on retrieval. On difficult problems, they rely primarily on back-up strategies. This can be seen in Fig. 2.1. The more difficult the problem, defined here in terms of percentage of errors, the more often children use back-up strategies.

Comparing children's behavior under conditions where they are allowed to use back-up strategies to that under conditions where they are not allowed to use them reveals just how adaptive the children's strategy choices are. Children perform more accurately on all problems when allowed to use back-up strategies. However, they use back-up strategies most often where such strategies do them the most good. That is, on problems where children's percent correct is much higher on back-up strategy trials than on retrieval trials, they use backup strategies very often. On problems where percent correct is only slightly higher when children use backup strategies, they use them much less often (Siegler, 1987a).

This pattern of strategy use allows children to strike an effective balance between concerns of speed and accuracy. They use the fastest strategy, retrieval, most often on problems where they can do so accurately, and use slower back-up strategies when they are necessary for accurate performance.

Children make comparably adaptive choices among alternative back-up strategies. Consider choices between the min strategy and the sum strategy (counting from 1). Although counting from the larger addend might appear to always be more efficient than counting from 1, most kindergarteners and first graders use both strategies. One reason may be that children find it easier to start counting at 1 than at an arbitrary point higher than 1 (Fuson, Richards, & Briars, 1982). Especially when the amount of counting to be done is relatively large, it may be difficult to start from a number other than 1 and keep track of both the amount of counting that has been done and the amount that remains to be done. In any case, children most frequently use the min strategy, and least frequently use the sum strategy on problems

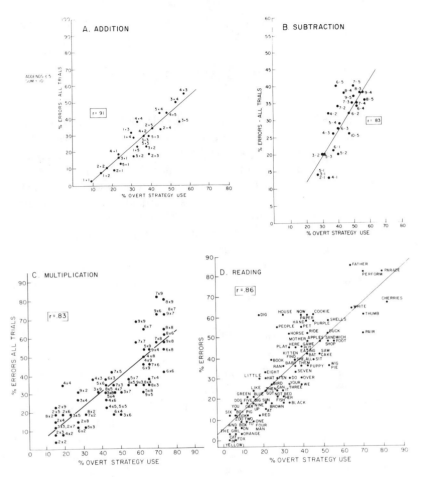

FIG. 2.1. Correlations between percent overt strategy use and percent errors on addition, subtraction, multiplication, and word identification problems.

such as 9 + 2, where the difference between the two addends is large and/or where the size of the smaller addend is small (Siegler, 1987b). This pattern makes sense. The greater the difference between the two addends, the greater the savings in number of counts that the min strategy provides over the sum strategy. The smaller the size of the smaller addend, the easier it is to execute the min strategy correctly. Thus, children behave adaptively both in choosing among alternative back-up strategies and in choosing between stating a retrieved answer and using a back-up strategy. The question is how they make such adaptive choices.

THE DISTRIBUTIONS OF ASSOCIATIONS MODEL

Siegler and Shrager (1984) developed the distributions of associations model to account for strategy choices in preschoolers' addition and subtraction. Since then, the model has been extended to kindergarteners' and first graders' subtraction (Siegler, 1987a), third and fourth graders' multiplication (Siegler, 1988a), second and third graders' spelling (Siegler, 1986), first graders' word identification (Siegler, 1988b), and second and third graders' time-telling (Siegler & McGilly, 1989). Our research group is currently in the process of developing a more intelligent second-generation model that will have the capabilities of the original model and a number of others as well. In the next section we describe both models, first the distribution-of-associations model and then the new strategy choice model.

Representation and Process

The two main parts of the distributions-of-associations model are a representation of knowledge about particular problems and a process that operates on this representation to produce answers. The answers, in turn, reshape the knowledge in the representation; the model learns by doing. Thus, factors that influence which answers are generated on a particular trial also determine the later contents of the knowledge representation. Back-up strategies, knowledge of related numerical operations, and frequency of encountering problems all contribute to development through their influence on current behavior.

First consider the representation. As shown in Fig. 2.2, children are hypothesized to associate responses, both correct and incorrect, with specific problems. For example, 3 + 5 would be associated not only with 8 but also with 6, 7, and 9. The representations of particular problems can be classified along a dimension of the *peakedness* of their distribution of associations. In a peaked distribution, such as that on the left in Fig. 2.2, most of the associative strength is concentrated in a single answer, ordinarily the correct answer. At the other extreme, in a flat distribution, such as that on the right of Fig. 2.2, associative strength is dispersed among several answers, with none of them forming a strong peak.

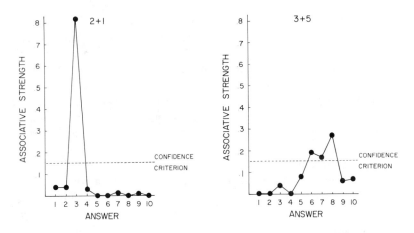

FIG. 2.2. Peaked (left) and flat (right) distributions of associations.

The process that operates on this representation involves three sequential phases, any one of which can produce an answer and thus terminate the process: retrieval, elaboration of the representation, and application of an algorithm. The model indicates that when trying to add numbers, a girl might first try to retrieve an answer; if not sufficiently confident of any answer, she might elaborate her representation of the problem by putting up fingers corresponding to the two addends, to see if she recognized how many fingers there were; if she still did not know the answer, she might count the fingers and advance as the answer the number corresponding to the last count. All distributions-of-associations models include these three sequential phases. The way in which retrieval occurs is also constant across the models, although the details of the other two phases are specific to each task.

The way in which the retrieval process works is central within the model. Probability of retrieving any given answer to a problem is proportional to that answer's associative strength relative to the total associative strengths of all answers to the problem. For example, if a given answer had an associative strength of .4, and the total associative strength of all answers was .8, then that answer would be retrieved on 50% of retrieval efforts.

Once retrieved, an answer is stated if its associative strength exceeds a response threshold known as the *confidence criterion*. In Fig. 2.2, the confidence criterion is depicted as being at .15. Thus, if a girl had a distribution of associations and a confidence criterion like that shown for 3 + 5 in Fig. 2.2, she would state a retrieved answer if she retrieved 6, 7, or 8, but not if she retrieved any other answer.[1] If the associative strength of the answer that is retrieved does not exceed the confidence criterion, the child can again retrieve an answer from the problem's distribution of associations and state it if its associative strength exceeds the confidence criterion. If the retrieval process fails to yield a statable answer within the allocated number of searches, the child generates an answer by using a back-up strategy, such as the min or sum strategy.

As discussed in previous articles (e.g., Siegler & Shrager, 1984), this model accounts for a broad range of children's behavior in solving arithmetic problems. Among these are which strategies children use, their frequency of errors and lengths of solution times on different problems, and the particular errors that they make. To illustrate the model's workings, consider its account of how children come to use back-up strategies most often on the most difficult problems. The reason suggested by the model is that the same factor that determines problem difficulty also determines whether retrieval or a back-up strategy is used. This factor is the peakedness of the problem's distribution of associations. To understand this interpretation, it is useful to compare the model's workings on problems with peaked and flat distributions of associations.

Relative to a peaked distribution, a flat distribution will elicit a higher percentage of use of back-up strategies (because flat distributions, by definition, lack a strongly associated answer that has a high probability of being retrieved and a high probability of exceeding the confidence criterion once it is retrieved; the absence of such a strongly associated answer will lead to children not being able to state any retrieved answer and instead using a back-up strategy). The flat distribution will also elicit a higher percentage of errors (because differences between the strengths of associations with the problem of correct and incorrect answers are by definition smaller in the flatter

---

[1]Within the model, the confidence criterion is set randomly and independently on each trial. It might be .15 on one trial, .70 on another, and .40 on a third. This variability in confidence criteria was critical in accounting for the trial-to-trial variability whereby a child would use retrieval one day on a problem and the min strategy the next day on the same problem. Presumably, a more intelligent criterion-setting process could only improve the model's performance. However, there was no evidence for such intelligent selection of confidence criteria. The point of letting the criterion-setting process be random was to demonstrate that the model would produce adaptive strategy choices even without an intelligent, criterion-setting mechanism.

distribution). Finally, the flatter distribution will lead to longer solution times (because the flatter the distribution, the less likely that an answer whose associative strength exceeds the confidence criterion will be retrieved and stated on an early retrieval attempt).

Thus, within this model, back-up strategies are used primarily on the most difficult problems, because the peakedness of the distribution of associations determines both problem difficulty and frequency of use of backup strategies.

Changes in the Representation With Practice

How do some problems come to have more peaked distributions than others? The model's basic assumption here is that people associate whatever answer they state, correct or incorrect, with the problem on which they state it. This assumption reduces the issue of what factors lead children to develop a particular distribution of associations on each problem to the more tractable issue of what factors lead them to state particular answers on each problem.

Three factors that seem to influence children's answers to arithmetic problems are difficulty of executing back-up strategies on the problem, frequency of encountering the problem, and knowledge of related numerical operations. Consider how each of them affects preschoolers' addition.

Difficulty of Correctly Executing Back-Up Strategies. One influence on which problems come to have peaked distributions is the difficulty of executing back-up strategies. Because the main back-up strategy that preschoolers use to add is the sum strategy, the sum of the addends provides a good measure of the relative difficulty of different problems solved in this way. The more objects children need to represent, and the more objects they then need to count, the more likely they are to err (Gelman & Gallistel, 1978). Thus, problems with large sums are harder to learn than problems with small sums, because on the large-sum problems, children are more likely to err in their counting. Such errors increase associations between the problem and incorrect answers rather than increasing the problem's association with the correct answer.

Exposure to Problems. A second influence on acquisition of distributions of associations is amount of exposure to each problem. Parents, teachers, and textbooks present some problems more often than others. The more exposures to a problem, the more opportunities the child has to associate the correct answer with it. As long as the correct answer is produced more often than any single incorrect answer, more frequent problem presentation will lead to faster acquisition of peaked distributions of associations.

To examine the pattern of input in preschoolers' addition, Siegler and Shrager (1984) invited 30 parents of 2- to 4-year-olds to teach their children to solve addition problems as they might at home. The purpose was to see how often parents presented each problem.

The parents' presentations of problems helped explain several otherwise anomalous results. Numerous investigators have found that ties (e.g., 3 + 3, 6 + 6) are easier than the sizes of their smaller addend would suggest (Groen & Parkman, 1972; Siegler & Robinson, 1982; Svenson, 1975). Parents presented ties considerably more than other problems. Investigators also have found that "+1" problems such as 3 + 1 and 4 + 1 are easier than the corresponding "1+" problems, such 1 + 3 and 1 + 4 (Groen & Parkman, 1972; Siegler & Robinson, 1982; Svenson, 1975). Parents presented "+1" problems 5 times as often as the corresponding "1+" problems.

Related Knowledge.   Most 4- and 5-year-olds know how to count quite well. This knowledge appears to both help and hurt their addition performance. Counting helps by providing a back-up strategy to use when children cannot retrieve a statable answer. It can also hurt, however, by interfering with efforts to retrieve correct answers. This is illustrated by children's performance on ascending series problems (items on which the second addend is larger than the first, such as 2 + 3 and 3 + 5). On all six of these problems that were included in two separate experiments in Siegler and Shrager (1984), the most frequent error made by 4- and 5-year-olds was to say that the answer was the number one greater than the second addend (Fig. 2.3). That is, they answered that 2 + 3 = 4 and 3 + 5 = 6. The result suggested that such problems triggered associations with children's knowledge of the counting string. Ironically, on "1 + N" problems, such as 1 + 3 and 1 + 4, such counting associations would help children state the correct answers. To the extent that answers become associated with the problems on which they are stated, these counting associations would interfere with building of a peaked distribution of associations on problems such as 2 + 3 and would contribute positively to the process on problems such as 1 + 3.

Stepwise multiple regression analyses have been used to determine

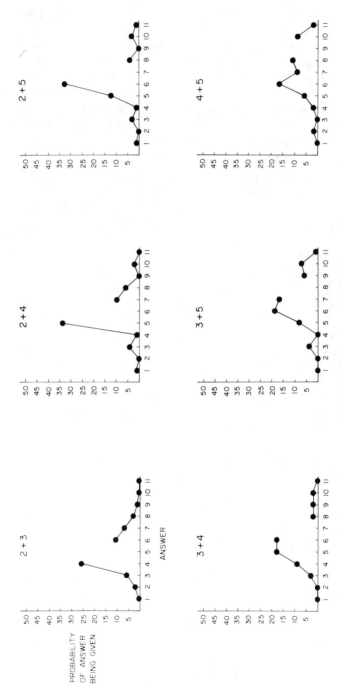

FIG. 2.3. Percent of particular errors on ascending series problems.

35

the independent and combined effects of these three variables on the peakedness of each problem's distribution of associations. For example, the regression analysis of preschoolers' addition performance on each problem included as predictor variables the sum of the addends on the problem (corresponding to the difficulty of executing the sum strategy on that problem); whether the problem included an interfering counting association, a helpful one, or none at all; and the frequency with which parents presented that problem to their child. The variable being predicted was the peakedness of each problem's distribution of associations. This was operationally defined as the percentage of trials on which children retrieved the correct answer in experiments where time limits precluded them from using any strategy other than retrieval (see Siegler, 1987a, 1988a; Siegler & Shrager, 1984, for details).

All three factors hypothesized to contribute to the development of the distribution of associations have been found to contribute to the peakedness of the distributions and the particular errors that were made. For example, in preschoolers' addition, the three variables together accounted for 85% of the variance in the peakedness of different problems' distributions of associations (Siegler & Shrager, 1984). The size of the sum was the first variable to enter the regression and accounted for 68% of the variance, the counting-associations variable entered next and accounted for an additional 10%, and the parental-input variable added 7% more. Together, the three variables accounted for at least 80% of the variance in the peakedness of different problems' distributions of associations in preschoolers' addition, kindergarteners' and first graders' subtraction, and third and fourth graders' multiplication.

Computer Simulations

Operating Procedures. We also have built computer simulations of the learning of addition, subtraction, and multiplication in which these three hypothesized influences on development play a central role (Siegler, 1987a; 1988a; Siegler & Shrager, 1984).[2] The basic operating procedures of the simulations, together with their specific realizations within the simulation of preschoolers' addition, are listed here.

---

[2]Jeff Shrager and Chris Shipley deserve tremendous credit for writing the code, compiling the simulations' output, and relating the output to children's behavior.

1. The simulation was presented problems in accord with their relative frequency in parental input or textbooks. Within the simulation of preschoolers' addition, this involved presenting the 25 problems with addends between 1 and 5 in accord with their relative frequency in the parental input study previously described.

2. Before each problem, the simulation generated a confidence criterion, with the criterion varying randomly from one problem to the next within the range of possible associative strengths.

3. Probability of retrieving an answer was proportional to that answer's associative strength relative to the associative strengths of all answers to the problem. A retrieved answer was stated if its associative strength exceeded the confidence criterion on that trial. Retrieval attempts continued until either the associative strength of a retrieved answer exceeded the confidence criterion or the number of searches for a retrievable answer matched the number that were allowed.

4. If no answer had yet been stated, the program generated an elaborated representation. In the case of preschoolers' addition, the main elaboration corresponded to putting up fingers. Once the elaborated representation was generated, the model temporarily (for the duration of the trial) added a constant to the associative strength of the answer that equalled the number of objects being represented. This temporary strengthening was analogous to kinesthetic or visual cues from the elaborated representation adding associative strength to that answer. Then an answer was retrieved in the standard way and the answer stated if its associative strength exceeded the confidence criterion.

5. If no answer had yet been stated, the model used an algorithmic back-up strategy. This algorithmic strategy always yielded a statable answer. In the case of preschoolers' addition, the algorithmic strategy was counting the objects in the elaborated representation (e.g., counting fingers).

6. Every time the simulation advanced an answer, the association between that answer and the problem increased. The increment was twice as great for correct answers, that presumably were reinforced, as for incorrect answers, that presumably were not.

The Simulation's Behavior.   The simulation ran in two phases: a learning phase and a test phase. The learning phase was designed to resemble children's experience with addition prior to the time at which

A

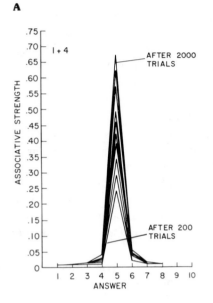

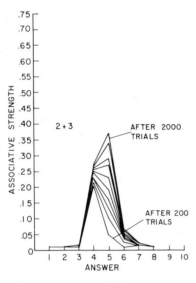

B

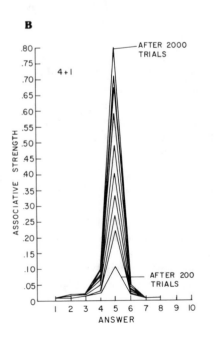

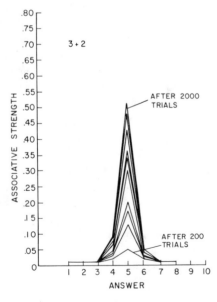

38

c

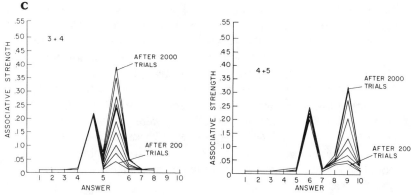

FIG. 2.4. Computer simulation's output on problems differing only on (a) type of counting association; (b) frequency of presentation; and (c) sums.

they entered the experiment. The test phase was intended to resemble behavior in the experimental setting, given children's prior experience. Again, we provide specifics for the model of preschoolers' addition.

The learning phase included 2,000 trials, an average of 80 for each of the 25 problems. During this period, children acquired more or less peaked distributions of associations on each problem. As discussed previously, three variables shaped the learning process: associations from the counting string, frequency of presentation of each problem, and the difficulty of executing back-up strategies.

To highlight the contribution of each of these variables, Siegler and Shrager (1984) compared pairs of problems that differed on that variable but whose status was the same on the other two variables. First consider 1 + 4 and 2 + 3, problems that have identical sums and frequencies of presentation, but one with a helpful and one with an interfering association from the counting string. As shown in Fig. 2.4A, the item that has the helpful association, 1 + 4, rapidly built a peak at the answer 5. The association between the item with the interfering association, 2 + 3, and the answer 5 started from a lower point and grew more slowly. At the end of the learning phase, after 2,000 trials, the answer 5 had 77% of the total associative strength for 1 + 4 versus 46% for 2 + 3. The peak for 1 + 4 also was higher in absolute terms: .67 versus .37. The greater percentage of total associative strength at 5 for 1 + 4 means that the simulation was more likely to retrieve 5 on this problem. The higher absolute peak for 1 + 4 means that the simulation would state 5 on a higher percentage of trials where it retrieved it.

Figure 2.4B illustrates the developmental course for two problems that have identical sums and that lack counting string associations, but that differ in frequency of presentation. The problem 4 + 1 was presented on 5.4% of trials, whereas the problem 3 + 2 was presented on 3.7%. The presentation rate had a marked effect on how high the peak rose as well as some effect on how peaked the distribution was. After 2,000 trials, the absolute associative strength of the peak for 4 + 1 was .80, whereas for 3 + 2 the associative strength was .51. The percentages of associative strength that were located in the peak answer were 76% and 69% respectively. These differences indicate that 4 + 1 would be retrieved somewhat more often than 3 + 2, and would be stated on a considerably higher percentage of those trials on which it was retrieved.

Finally, as shown in Fig. 2.4C, the sum exerted an effect even when the frequency of presentation and the type of counting string association was constant. The problems 3 + 4 and 4 + 5 were identical in frequency of presentation and in having interfering counting association. However, they differed in their sums. The peak of the item with the lower sum rose more rapidly and at the end of 2,000 learning trials was higher (.39 vs. .32) than the peak for the item with the higher sum. The distribution also was more peaked, with the peak for 3 + 4 having 50% of the total associative strength and the peak for 4 + 5 having 43%. Thus, all three variables influenced the percentage of trials on which the correct answer was retrieved and the probability that it was stated once it was retrieved.

After the simulation completed the learning phase, it proceeded to the test phase. Where the learning phase was intended to model children's experience prior to the experiment, the test phase was intended to parallel their experience in the experiment. The test phase differed from the learning phase in only two respects. First, to parallel the empirical experiments that were conducted, all problems were presented equally often in the test phase. Second, because each child who participated in the empirical experiments received only two exposures to each problem, thereby providing very little opportunity to learn, the asociative strengths remained constant throughout the phase. The goal was to model a large number of children, each having a brief experimental session, rather than a single child having a very long session.

The simulation's behavior in the test phase closely resembled that of children in Siegler and Robinson (1982) and Siegler and Shrager (1984). It generated the four strategies that the children used. The relative solution times of the simulation's strategies also were identical to those produced by the children. The simulation's errors also were like the children's; for example, its most frequent error on all six ascending problems was the answer one greater than the second addend.

Most important, the simulation's performance resembled that of the children in which problems elicited the greatest percentage of errors, which took the longest to answer, and which elicited the highest percentage of backup strategies. As shown in Table 2.3, all of the correlations of greatest interest between the simulation's behavior and that of the children exceeded $r = .85$. Moreover, the intrasimulation correlations among percentage of errors on retrieval trials, percentage of back-up strategy use, and mean solution times on retrieval trials on each problem all exceeded $r = .90$.

In summary, a computer simulation that took into account difficulty of executing back-up strategies, frequency of problem presentation, and effects of related knowledge was able to simulate a wide range of phenomena that characterize children's arithmetic. The simulation both performed and learned. At the outset, its performance was slow, inaccurate, and heavily dependent on back-up strategies. With experience, its performance became faster and more accurate, and retrieval increasingly replaced back-up strategies. The simulation found the same problems difficult that children did and made the same types of strategy choices on them that children did. In short, the simulation demonstrated that the underlying model was sufficient to generate a wide range of behavior that children show in arithmetic.

Table 2.3
Computer Simulation's Performance

Intramodel Correlations

$r_{\text{\% errors and \% overt strategy use}} = .97$

$r_{\text{\% errors and } \bar{x} \text{ solution times}} = .97$

$r_{\text{\% overt strategy use and } \bar{x} \text{ solution times}} = .99$

Correlations Between Children's and Model's Behavior[a]

$r_{\text{\% errors produced by model and children}} = .88$

$r_{\text{\% overt strategy use produced by model and children}} = .92$

$r_{\bar{x} \text{ solution times produced by model and children}} = .87$

[a]Children's data are combined results of retrieval trials in Siegler and Robinson and in replication condition of Siegler and Shrager.

THE NEW STRATEGY CHOICE MODEL

Although it had many strengths, the distributions of associations model also had clear limitations. It was inflexible, in the sense that it always tried to retrieve first and only would attempt a back-up strategy after efforts to retrieve failed. Its knowledge was problem-specific; regardless of whether it had previously learned 2 or 92 problems, its approach to a new problem was identical. It modeled in detail the choice between stating a retrieved answer and using a back-up strategy, but not choices between alternative back-up strategies.

The new strategy-choice model was developed to overcome these limitations while preserving the strengths of the original model. The basic approach was to generalize the principles on which the model was based along two dimensions: the types of choices that were made and the types of data that were considered in making the choices. With regard to the types of choices that were made, the original model's procedure for choosing among answers was generalized to choosing among strategies as well as answers. With regard to the types of data that were considered, the database was extended to include not only the answers that the model had previously generated but also the speeds and accuracies that each strategy had produced.

Figure 2.5 illustrates the general organization of the new model. As in the original distributions of associations model, the new model includes a representation and a process. The representation includes connections not only between problems and answers but also between strategies and specific problems, strategies and particular types of problems, and strategies and the class of problems as a whole. These connections become stronger or weaker depending on the speed and

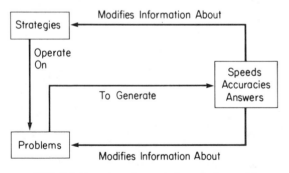

FIG. 2.5. Overview of new strategy choice model.

accuracy that the strategy has generated in previous uses on the class of problems as a whole; on problems having certain features, such as smaller addends of particular sizes; and on particular problems.

In addition to information about speed and accuracy, the representation of each strategy also includes *novelty points*. This aspect of the representation arose through attempts to face a problem that is probably quite general: How do new strategies ever get used in situations where existing strategies work reasonably well? The simulation deals with this problem by assigning novelty points to newly discovered strategies. These novelty points temporarily add to the strength of the new strategies and thus allow them to be tried even when they have little or no track record. With each use of the new strategy, some of its novelty points are lost, but information about its effectiveness is gained, so that the strategy's effectiveness increasingly determines how often and when it is used. The novelty points idea was motivated by the view that people are often interested in exercising newly acquired cognitive capabilities (Piaget, 1970) and by the realization that without a track record, a newly developed strategy might otherwise never be chosen, especially if previously developed strategies had been reasonably successful.

The novelty points contribute to the representation in much the same way as the speed and accuracy the strategy has previously generated. The initial number of novelty points is set as a percentage of the total associative strength of all strategies already associated with the problem. For purposes of selecting a strategy, these novelty points are equivalent to the strategy having strength equal to the number of novelty points. Thus, if the number of novelty points of a new strategy is 5% of the total associative strength of all strategies and answers, the new strategy has a 5% probability of being selected. Unlike the usual associative strengths, however, the novelty points decrease with each use of the strategy. If the strategy leads to quick and accurate responding, the associative strength that it gains more than offsets the amount lost through the decrease in novelty points. If it generates inaccurate and/or slow responding on the trial, the novelty points are gradually used up without compensating gains in strength.

Now we can consider the new simulation's process for operating on the representation and producing performance. The process involves two phases; strategy choice and strategy execution. Within the strategy-choice phase, strategies are retrieved with probability proportional to their strength relative to the strength of all of the strategies. These strengths are based on each strategy's speed and accuracy in the domain, its speed and accuracy on the specific problem (if such information exists), and its speed and accuracy on problems having similar characteristics (e.g., similar first addend sizes, similar smaller addend sizes).

Once a strategy is chosen, the model attempts to execute it. If the strategy can be executed, it is used to generate an answer. If it cannot be executed (for example, if retrieval is chosen but no answer with associative strength exceeding the confidence criterion can be retrieved), the process returns to the strategy-choice phase. The cycle continues until the model chooses a strategy that can be executed, at which point it executes that strategy and produces the answer.

The simulation learns about the characteristics of strategies and problems by using the strategies to solve the problems. As in the previous version of the simulation, each statement of an answer increases the association between the problem and that answer. Beyond this, the new simulation keeps records concerning the speed and accuracy produced by each strategy across all problems and on each individual problem. Specifically, whenever a strategy is used to solve a problem, the speed with which the solution was generated and the correctness or incorrectness of the answer are added to the databases concerning the strategy in general and the strategy's usefulness on the particular problem. In this way, the simulation comes to know the general speed and accuracy of each strategy as well as where the strategy works most effectively.

The speed and accuracy with which each strategy can solve a given problem are functions of the number of counts needed to solve the problem using that strategy. For example, solving 9 + 1 would require 1 count if the min strategy was used and 10 counts if the sum strategy was used. Because counting from an arbitrary point greater than 1 is more difficult than counting from 1, solution times and errors increase more rapidly with each count when the min strategy is used than when the sum strategy is. Thus, within the simulation as within children's performance, the min strategy's advantage is greatest on problems such as 9 + 1, where the min strategy can solve the problem with little counting and where the sum strategy requires many more counts.

We are still in the process of perfecting the new simulation, but it seems to be working well. It produces learning and performance much like those of children. For example, on its most recent run, its performance progressed from 55% correct early in the run to 98%

correct at the end. Its use of retrieval progressed from 16% early in the run to 99% at the end. It also chose strategies in an adaptive fashion. Overall, on the 81 addition problems with addends between 1 and 9, its percent errors, mean solution time, and percent use of retrieval all correlated at least $r = .80$ with the peakedness of children's distribution of associations on that problem (with peakedness defined as in the previous simulation).

The new simulation went beyond the previous one in several ways. It chose sensibly among alternative backup strategies. For example, it used the min strategy most often on problems such as 9 + 1, where the difference between the addends was large and the amount of counting required by the size of the smaller addend was small. It used the sum strategy most often on problems such as 9 + 8, where both retrieval and the min strategy are difficult to execute correctly. Further, the new simulation generalized its knowledge of strategies and how they work on various types of problems to problems it had never encountered previously. It was able to make reasonable projections about which strategy would be most effective on the basis of its experience on related problems. Thus, the new simulation seems a promising way to extend the previous modeling of children's strategy choices.

Construction of New Strategies

An issue addressed by neither the earlier model nor the new one is how new strategies are constructed. The emphasis has been on how children select among strategies they already know, rather than on how they add new strategies to their repertoire. The experiment reported in this book was undertaken to provide a database about the construction of new strategies, as well as to suggest ideas about how the acquisition process occurs.

A previous study (Groen & Resnick, 1977) demonstrated the feasibility of studying construction of the min strategy. Initially, 4-year-olds who had not yet learned to add were taught the sum strategy. Once they mastered it, they were given extensive practice on single-digit addition problems: two sessions per week over a 3- to 5-month period. Each child's mean solution time on each problem was calculated for each successive block of five sessions. These data, in turn, were used to infer the best predictor of solution times on each problem at different points in the study. If the best predictor of each problem's mean RT was its sum, the child would be viewed as using the sum strategy. If the best predictor was the size of the smaller addend, the child would be viewed as using the min strategy. The central issue was whether children would invent the min strategy despite never having been taught it.

Some of the children did meet the criterion for use of the min strategy. In particular, the best predictor of 5 of the 10 children's solution times shifted from the size of the sum to the size of the smaller addend. Groen and Resnick concluded that these children were "no longer using the (sum) algorithm they were taught" because they had "invented a more efficient procedure (the min strategy)" (p. 645).

Neches (1987; Resnick & Neches, 1984) noted that it is very difficult to actually observe a child in the process of inventing the min strategy and concluded that "in the absence of any direct observation of the process of discovering MIN, one way to proceed in attempting to account for it is to build a self-modifying system that begins with SUM and, without any additional external input, changes to use of MIN (Resnick & Neches, 1984, p. 278). Neches' model indicated that children rely sequentially on four strategies. In the initial strategy, they count out objects corresponding to the first addend, count out objects corresponding to the second addend, and count the objects in both sets together (i.e., on 2 + 3, they would count "1, 2", "1, 2, 3", "1, 2, 3, 4, 5"). Next, they notice that the first set of objects is being counted twice, and switch to first counting out objects corresponding to each set and then counting from the number corresponding to the first addend (on 2 + 3, they would count "1, 2", "1, 2, 3", "2, 3, 4, 5"). Following this, they notice that they could start counting from the first addend and do so (on 2 + 3, they would count "2, 3, 4, 5"). Finally they compare the amount of counting they are doing on inverse problems (e.g., 2 + 3 and 3 + 2) and move from always counting from the first addend to counting from whichever addend is larger (on 2 + 3, they would count "3, 4, 5").

Both Groen and Resnick's data and Neches' model are intriguing, but both leave much unknown about the strategy construction process. A problem that they share is the assumption that children use a single strategy at a time. As we have seen, this assumption is incorrect for both 4-year-olds and older children. Children continue to use the sum strategy after they have discovered the min strategy, and use a variety of other strategies before, after, and during the invention of the min strategy. Further, the Neches model shows a certain amount of prescience that children are unlikely to share. Within the model, children compare the effort involved in counting inverse problems such as 2 + 3 and 3 + 2 and use their observations to conclude that they should count from the larger addend rather than from the first one. How do they know to compare these inverse problems? Neches suggested that they note that the answers to the problems are the same. If this is the case how do they know not to compare the effort needed to count on other problems, such as 2 + 3 and 1 + 4? Alternatively, if they were hypothesized to make the comparison because they understand commutativity, where did the understanding come from, and why did it not yield the discovery until the second and third strategies had been used?

A further issue concerns methods for studying the strategy construction process. Differences between the ideas expressed in Neches' model and the empirical data that emerged from the Groen and Resnick study underline the importance of analyzing strategy use on a trial-by-trial basis. Both of the transitional phases in Neches' model emphasize counting from the first addend. Groen and Resnick explicitly noted that they failed to find evidence that children ever used this approach.

This lack of supporting evidence, however, may have been due to limitations of the chronometric analyses they employed, rather than to children not using the strategy. Groen and Resnick inferred which strategy children used from the best predictor of solution times on blocks of 125 trials. As noted earlier, this approach is reasonable if children only use a single strategy during the trial block. However, if children counted from the first addend only on some problems, or only used the strategy briefly, the strategy might well not show up in analyses of solution times averaged over many trials. Thus, the strategies that Neches postulated might not show up even if his ideas about their roles are entirely correct. The same holds true for any other short-lived or sporadically used transitional strategy that children may have constructed prior to their discovery of the min strategy. We hoped that by assessing strategy use on a trial-by-trial basis, we would be able to detect any such fleeting transitional strategies that children used, as well as being present when each child discovered the min strategy.

3

A Study of Strategy Construction

Our plan for studying strategy construction was quite simple. Children were first given a pretest. The purpose was to identify individuals who did not yet know the min strategy but who did know other strategies for solving addition problems. Then, those children whose pretest performance met our criteria participated in a practice phase, during which they received extensive experience solving addition problems. The hope was that with sufficient experience, the children would discover the min strategy and would generalize it to some degree to new problems.

The plan involved two main risks. One was that children would not be able to discover the min strategy when given this type and amount of experience. The other was that children would find it trivially easy to construct the new strategy. In either case, we would not be able to examine long-term strategy construction.

Fortunately, neither of these potential problems arose. Most children did discover the min strategy, thus allowing us to examine the conditions leading up to the discovery, the discovery itself, and the way in which children generalized the new strategy to other problems. On the other hand, discovery of the strategy was far from easy. Among the eight children who completed the experiment, two first used the new strategy in the last week of the practice phase, and another child never did use it. Thus, the strategy discovery process was of the type that we were interested in examining — one that required more time and experience than a typical single session experiment would allow, but also one where the strategy discoveries would come while we were young enough to enjoy them.

In the course of conducting the study, we learned a lot about microgenetic methods. One of the primary lessons was the difficulty of maintaining precise control on experimental procedures in such studies. Due to a minor epidemic of colds, variations in children's schedules, waxing and waning of their enthusiasm for participating, and a host of other factors that arose from February to May, some children received more problems than others. Also, because some children simply could not cope with some of the problems, and because their continued participation in the experiment demanded that they not become too frustrated, the types of problems that they received varied to some degree. These types of difficulties are probably inherent to studies that require continuous participation of children over several month periods. Although the difficulties should not be minimized, they still seem to us to be an acceptable cost for the richness and precision of observation that the microgenetic approach allows.

METHOD

Pretest Phase

Subject Selection. A pretest was used to select children for participation in the practice phase of the experiment. The goal of the pretesting was to identify children who did not already know the min strategy but who possessed a reasonable degree of skill in adding numbers. Assessments were based on children's overt problem-solving activity on 20 simple addition problems, on their immediately retrospective reports of how they had solved the problems, and on the strategies for solving addition problems that they recommended to a hypothetical younger child.

To participate in the practice phase, children needed to meet a number of criteria. They could not report on any of the 20 pretest addition problems that they had used the min strategy or any other strategy that involved counting from a number greater than one. None of their visible or audible behavior could suggest that they had counted from a number greater than 1. When explaining to a hypothetical younger child how to add 2 + 4, they could not recommend the min strategy or any other strategy involving counting from a number greater than 1. The size of the smaller addend could not be the best predictor of their solution times on the 20 addition problems. To assure that they had reasonable knowledge of addition strategies other than the min approach, they also needed to answer correctly on at least 50% of the addition problems.

All of these criteria were met by 8 of the 29 4- and 5-year-olds who took the pretest. Because this sample was a little smaller than we wanted, and because we were worried about potential dropouts, we added two children who met all but one of the previously listed criteria. One girl met all criteria except that her percent correct was too low. She was trained to execute the sum strategy until her use of it seemed sufficiently accurate. Another girl met all criteria except that the size of the smaller addend was the best predictor of her solution times. This child was included because she never reported using the min strategy, never gave any overt sign of using it, and did not recommend it as a way of solving 2 + 4. Also, although the size of the smaller addend was the best predictor of her solution times, it accounted for only 28% of the variance in them.

Among the 10 children who were thus selected, 8 completed the entire 11-week practice phase. One child did not finish because she took the experiment so seriously that she became upset when she answered incorrectly. The other child did not finish because of the opposite problem; he gave extensive evidence of not trying. All of the analyses reported here are based on the eight children who completed the entire experiment.

These eight children, five girls and three boys, attended a preschool in the Pittsburgh area. Their mean age at the beginning of the experiment was 60 months, with a range of 52 to 68 months. All were from middle- or upper middle-class families. Among them, four were in a kindergarten class and four were in a pre-kindergarten class. Both before and during the experiment, the kindergartners received some exposure to arithmetic problems with sums below 30 as part of their daily routine. They were taught to solve these problems by counting out sets of plastic counters to represent each addend and then counting the total number of counters on the table. The prekindergartners received no classroom instruction in arithmetic prior to or during the experiment. Two experimenters conducted both the pretest and the succeeding phases of the experiment. One was a 24-year-old male graduate student (the second author); the other was a 21-year-old female undergraduate.

Problems and Procedure. The main purpose of the pretest was to identify children who did not yet know the min strategy but who were reasonably adept in adding by use of other strategies. A second purpose was to assess children's knowledge of numerical magnitudes and counting, so that we could examine the relation between initial skill on these tasks and subsequent discovery and generalization of the min strategy in the practice phase.

The pretest was presented in four sessions, on days as close to consecutive as possible given constraints of the children's schedules. In each pretest session, as in all subsequent parts of the experiment, children were presented problems individually in a laboratory room down the hall from their classroom. Within the room, they sat directly across a child-size table from the experimenter.

The first three pretest sessions began with addition problems. Over these sessions, each of the 20 non-tie items with addends between 1 and 5 inclusive was presented once. Here and in subsequent phases of the experiment, order of problem presentation was randomly generated for each child, subject to two constraints. One constraint was that no item could be followed by an item with the same addends in the opposite order (e. g., $5 + 3$ could not be followed by $3 + 5$). The other constraint was that no problem could be followed by another with one identical addend and the other addend within one of the corresponding addend in the preceding problem (e. g., $4 + 2$ could not be followed by $4 + 3$, $4 + 1$, $3 + 2$, or $5 + 2$). The goal was to minimize solutions based in whole or part on retrieving from short-term memory the answer to the immediately preceding problem.

Before each set of addition problems, children were instructed as follows:

We are going to do some addition problems today. I'll read a problem to you, and when you have an answer, tell me what it is. You can do anything you want to get the right answer, but try to answer the best that you can. You can just say the answer if you know it, or you can count or use your fingers or do whatever you want to do. It doesn't matter how you get the right answer—you don't even have to figure it out the same way every time—just as long as you try the best that you can.

After solving the first problem in the first session, the child was told the following:

I'm also interested in knowing how children your age figure out the answers to these problems. So, after you tell me each answer, I'm going to ask you how you figured out the answer. Tell me exactly what you did to figure out the answer.

The question "How did you figure out the answer to that problem?" was asked after each item, unless the child volunteered the information before being asked. If the child's description was unclear, the experimenter would ask follow-up questions. For example, if the child said only, "I counted," the experimenter would ask "How did you count?" If the child was unable to provide an explanation after this probe, the experimenter asked, "What number did you start counting on?" If the answer was completely unclear, the experimenter asked, "Did you count or did you already know the answer?"

Children frequently received general words of encouragement. Immediately after each correct answer, they were told that they were right and given a gold star. Immediately after incorrect answers, they were told that that answer was wrong and also told what the right answer was. After each problem, children attached the gold stars that they had won to a sheet of cardboard that constituted a permanent record of their performance.

Following the first set of addition problems, children were presented two strategy-recommendation questions. The first of these involved asking the child, "Suppose Spud (a Mr. Potato Head doll in the laboratory) is a littler kid than you are. Can you tell him a way to figure out the answer to one of the problems I just asked you, like 2 + 4?" Following the child's response, the experimenter asked the child the second strategy-recommendation question: "Do you know of any other ways you might tell Spud how to figure out how much 2 + 4 is?"

The fourth session was different from the first three, in that it involved presentation of numerical magnitude comparison and counting tasks. The numerical magnitude problems involved the 36 possible pairs of the digits 1–9 inclusive. On each trial, the child was asked which of two numbers was larger. The larger number was presented first on half of the trials. After these magnitude comparison questions, children were presented six tangible counting questions. These included two problems on which children needed to count out sets of objects, two on which they needed to count out a set of fingers while putting them up, and two on which they needed to count fingers that they already had put up. At the end, they were asked to count as high as they could.

Assessments of Solution Times and Strategies. Each child's behavior on the addition problems was recorded using a videocassette recorder and camera. The videotapes provided a useful supplement to children's verbal reports in cases where the explanations were unclear and in cases where the children's overt behavior contradicted their descriptions of what they had done.

Solution times were recorded through use of a digitizer, a device that prints digital times across the bottom of the taped scene. The times are accurate to one-tenth of a second, which seemed a sufficient degree of accuracy for the present task, where the median solution time was approximately 9 sec. Solution times were determined for each trial by subtracting the time when the experimenter finished stating the problem from the time when the child began to state the answer. If a child needed to have a problem repeated, the time subtracted was that following the final presentation of the problem. Similarly, if a child advanced more than one answer, the time associated with the final answer was used.

Strategy use on each addition problem was assessed by examining the videotaped record of overt behavior and the verbal self-report that was obtained immediately after the end of each trial. If no overt behavior was observed, the self-report was used as the basis of strategy classification on that trial. In cases where overt behavior differed from the child's self-report, the overt behavior was used to determine the strategy classification.

To examine the reliability of classification of the strategies, a research assistant and the second author independently rated children's strategies from the videotapes of 100 consecutive trials within the experiment. These trials included at least one session for each of the eight children in the experiment and at least one instance of each of the eight strategies that children were classified as using. The two raters' strategy assessments agreed on 95% of the trials that they examined. Thus, although the children were preschoolers, the combination of their overt behavior and immediately retrospective verbal reports led to highly reliable classification of their strategies.

One situation posed unavoidable difficulties in classifying the strategies. This was the situation where children counted from the first addend, and the first addend was also the larger addend. Such a situation would arise if children counted from 5 on 5 + 3, for example. Under such conditions, it was impossible to know from the behavior on that trial whether the strategy was best viewed as the min strategy or as counting from the first addend, since the two approaches would produce identical behavior.

The solution we adopted was to base decisions on the particular child's strategy use on problems where it was possible to discriminate (e.g., 3 + 5). Only one child ever counted from the first addend on such problems. Therefore, we classified the other children's counting from the first/larger addend on problems such as 5 + 3 as instances of the min strategy. For the one child who used both the min strategy and counting from the first addend on the trials where the two approaches produced different actions, we kept separate three types of behavior: unambiguous use of the min strategy, unambiguous use of counting from the first addend, and behavior consistent with both strategies.[1]

Practice Phase

The original plan was to repeatedly present the 20 non-tie problems with addends of 1 through 5 until all of the children discovered the min strategy. These were the types of problems on which we thought children were most likely to discover the min strategy. In particular, we hypothesized that children (and adults) most often discover new strategies in situations where they have available ample mental resources. With repeated exposure to small-addend problems, children would become increasingly able to retrieve answers, the mental

---

[1]It was logically possible that when children counted from the larger addend on problems with the smaller addend first, such as 2 + 5, they were following the strategy of counting from the second addend. However, the data gave no support for this view. As noted previously six of the seven children consistently counted from the larger addend whenever they counted from any number other than 1. The one child who sometimes counted from the first addend and sometimes from the larger addend never counted from the second addend when it was smaller, thus suggesting that she was not using a strategy of counting from the second addend. Thus, this logically possible strategy did not appear in children's performance.

resources required to solve the problems would decrease, and children would have sufficient unused mental resources to construct the new strategy. The logic was much like that of Case's (1985) theory. The possibility of comparing answers generated by the new strategy with answers that were already known also seemed likely to promote use of the min strategy once it was discovered.

We adhered to this procedure for the first 7 weeks of the practice phase. At the end of this period, however, we were not entirely satisfied with the number of children who had discovered the min strategy nor with how often the strategy was being used by children who had discovered it. This led us to consider a different perspective on the types of problems that would promote strategy discovery. The alternative view might be labeled the "necessity is the mother of invention" perspective. Within it, children would be expected to most often construct new strategies when their existing strategies were inadequate and when the new strategies would be much more effective.

This perspective led us to present to children in the eighth week of the practice phase a set of *challenge problems.* These challenge problems involved one addend greater than 10, typically in the low 20s, and one small addend, between 1 and 4. A representative challenge problem was $23 + 2$. Such problems were chosen because they would be impossible or extremely difficult to solve by either retrieval or counting from one, and because they would be much easier to solve via use of the min strategy. Thus, any child who discovered the min strategy or started to use it more often would benefit substantially in both speed and accuracy. To keep the children who had difficulty with these problems from becoming frustrated, occasional easier problems were mixed into the two sets of challenge problems. The problems in the two sets were $23 + 1$, $1 + 27$, $24 + 2$, $1 + 14$, $25 + 1$, $23 + 2$, $12 + 4$, $2 + 18$, $7 + 2$, $22 + 4$, $6 + 3$, $13 + 2$, $2 + 21$, $24 + 3$, and $15 + 3$.

In the 9th, 10th, and 11th weeks of the experiment, children received a mix of problem types. These included problems as easy as $3 + 1$ and problems as hard as $22 + 4$, with all gradations of difficulty in between. Presenting such a range of problems allowed a broader assessment of children's strategy choices than would have been possible with any single type of problem.

Overall, children received an average of 174 problems in the practice phase. Of these, an average of 126 were *small-addend problems* and 48 were *large-addend problems.* Within the set of large-addend problems, an average of 14 were challenge problems, that is problems that included one addend greater than 10, and 34 were not.

Small-addend problems were defined as problems with both addends between 1 and 5. Large-addend problems were defined as those with one addend of 6 or more, that is, problems where one of the addends could not be represented by the fingers on one hand. These two types of problems differed not only in addend size but also in how often and when they were presented. Small-addend problems were presented throughout the 11-week period (except for Week 8, when the challenge problems were presented), whereas large-addend problems were concentrated in Weeks 8–11. Because small-addend problems were presented throughout the experiment, performance on them provides the most realistic reflection of changes over time in children's speed, accuracy, and strategy use. Therefore, most analyses of changes over time focus on this set of problems.

As previously noted, variation in children's availability and enthusiasm resulted in considerable variability in the total number of problems and the number of problems of each type that children received. The total number of problems that children received varied from 130 to 244, the number of small-addend problems varied from 92 to 163, the number of large-addend problems varied from 29 to 81, and the number of challenge problems from 7 to 26. This child-by-child variability was one reason for the emphasis on individual children's performance in this, and especially in the next, chapter.

PRETEST RESULTS

The eight children who participated throughout the experiment answered correctly 68% of the pretest addition problems. As noted earlier, one of these children did not initially know how to add by counting from 1; she did not answer any of the pretest problems correctly. The other children's percent correct ranged from 65% to 100%, with a mean of 78% correct. Children most often used the sum strategy (43% of trials) and retrieval (34% of trials). Overall mean solution time was 9.8 sec with a median of 7.6 sec. Individual children's mean times ranged from 4.4 to 15.4 sec; medians ranged from 3.0 to 13.6 sec.

Children were very skillful at the magnitude comparison and

counting tasks that were included as possible predictors of later discovery of the min strategy. They answered correctly 93% of the magnitude comparison questions. Individual children's percent correct varied from 78% to 100%. Children also performed correctly on 90% of counting trials, with individuals ranging from 67% to 100% correct.

PRACTICE PHASE RESULTS

The remainder of this chapter is devoted to examining children's performance during the 11-week practice phase. The description is divided into four sections: an overview of children's performance in the experiment, discovery of the min strategy, changes that led up to the discovery, and generalization of the strategy to new problems.

Overview

The data of primary interest involved accuracy, speed, and strategy use.

Accuracy. As shown in Table 3.1, children correctly solved 85% of problems. They were correct on 89% of small-addend problems and 76% of large-addend ones. Individual children's accuracy ranged from 76% to 98%. All children answered the small-addend problems

TABLE 3.1
Overall Speed and Accuracy

	All Problems		Small-Addend Problems		Large-Addend Problems	
	% Correct	Median RT	% Correct	Median RT	% Correct	Median RT
Brittany	88	10.1	87	9.6	90	11.0
Christian	80	7.9	92	6.6	46	13.0
Danny	79	10.5	84	9.1	67	16.5
Jesse	95	9.9	97	10.0	90	8.8
Laine	76	8.5	83	7.9	42	23.2
Lauren	98	11.4	100	10.3	94	15.9
Ruth	83	8.3	81	8.4	85	8.0
Whitney	78	10.1	82	9.2	68	14.5
TOTAL	85	9.4	89	8.6	76	13.1

quite accurately, with individual children's percent correct ranging from 81% to 100%. There was much greater variability in accuracy on the large-addend problems, with individual children's percent correct ranging from 42% to 94%.

Children's performance became considerably more accurate over time. For purposes of comparison, their accuracy on the small-addend problems was grouped into five-session (35-problem) trial blocks. Their accuracy improved from 80% correct on the first trial block to 96% correct on the last one.[2]

Speed. The median solution time across all children and all problems was 9.4 sec (Table 3.1). The median for small addend problems was 8.6 sec, whereas that for large-addend problems was 13.1 sec.

Median solution times of individual subjects ranged from 7.9 sec to 11.4 sec. As with the accuracy data, variability of performance was considerably greater on the large-addend problems than on the small-addend ones. Individual children's median RTs ranged from 6.6 to 10.3 sec on the small-addend problems, but from 8.0 to 23.2 sec on the large-addend ones.

Children's times became faster during the study. Their mean RTs on small-addend problems (the only problems that were presented throughout the experiment) decreased from 11.1 sec in the first trial block to 9.3 sec in the last. The largest decreases in solution times came at the end of the experiment, following presentation of the challenge problems. During the first four trial blocks, times on small-addend problems decreased from 11.1 to 10.4 sec; during the last trial block, they decreased from 10.4 to 9.3 sec.

Strategy Use. Activities were classified into eight categories: the sum strategy, the min strategy, retrieval, finger recognition, guessing, counting from the first addend, decomposition, and the shortcut-sum strategy. Each strategy is described in Table 3.2. The first seven strategies in the list have been described in previous studies of young children's addition (e.g., Baroody & Ginsburg, 1986; Fuson, 1982; Ilg & Ames, 1951; Siegler & Robinson, 1982). However, the shortcut-sum

---

[2]Here and throughout the study, when children finished with one, two, or three sessions beyond the last completed trial block, the additional sessions were combined with the immediately-previous block. When there were four such additional sessions, they were counted as a new trial block.

TABLE 3.2
Children's Main Strategies

Strategy	Typical Use of Strategy to Solve $3+5$
Sum	Put up 3 fingers, put up 5 fingers, count fingers by saying "1,2,3,4,5,6,7,8."
Finger recognition	Put up 3 fingers, put up 5 fingers, say "8" without counting.
Short-cut sum	Say "1,2,3,4,5,6,7,8," perhaps simultaneously putting up one finger on each count.
Min	Say "5,6,7,8" or "6,7,8," perhaps simultaneously putting up one finger on each count beyond 5.
Count-from-first-addend	Say "3,4,5,6,7,8" or "4,5,6,7,8," perhaps simultaneously putting up one finger on each count.
Retrieval	Say an answer and explain it by saying "I just knew it."
Guessing	Say an answer and explain it by saying "I guessed."
Decomposition	Say "$3+5$ is like $4+4$, so it's 8."

strategy does not appear to have been recognized previously as a distinct approach. Because it was used quite often, and because it seemed to play an important role in the discovery of the min strategy, it seems worth describing in some detail.

The shortcut-sum strategy resembled the usual sum strategy in certain ways and the min strategy in others. On a problem such as 4 + 3, it involved counting "1, 2, 3, 4, 5, 6, 7" and answering "7." Thus, it was like the usual sum strategy in that it involved counting all of the numbers between one and the sum of the addends. However, it required only one count corresponding to each number, whereas the typical sum strategy required two counts of each (e.g., the sum strategy on 4 + 3 involved counting "1, 2, 3, 4 . . . 1, 2, 3 . . . 1, 2, 3, 4, 5, 6, 7").

Conversely, the shortcut-sum approach resembled the min strategy in that counting of the numbers that corresponded to the second addend began from a point greater than one. At times, it was also like the min strategy in that children would reverse the order of the addends so that the larger addend was first (e.g., on 3 + 4, they sometimes would count "1, 2, 3, 4 . . . 5, 6, 7." However, it was unlike the min strategy in that counting began at one rather than at the larger addend and in that counting often proceeded from the first addend even when it was smaller (e.g., on 3 + 4, children often would count "1, 2, 3 . . . 4, 5, 6, 7").

As shown in Table 3.3, the most frequently used strategies, in order of use, were sum, retrieval, shortcut-sum, finger recognition, and the

TABLE 3.3
Percent Use, Percent Correct, and Median RT for Each Strategy

Strategy	Percent Use	Percent Correct	Median RT
Sum	34	89	10.8
Retrieval	22	89	5.0
Short-cut sum	17	85	13.2
Finger recognition	11	92	6.4
Min	9	86	9.0
Guess	2	20	9.9
Count-from-first	1	40	15.6
Unknown	4	71	—
TOTAL	100	85	9.4

min strategy. Children used these five strategies on 93% of trials. All five yielded quite accurate performance, with percent correct ranging from 85% to 92%. The strategies did differ considerably in speed of execution. As in previous studies of preschoolers' and young elementary school children's addition (Siegler, 1987b; Siegler & Shrager, 1984), retrieval was the fastest strategy, finger recognition the next fastest, the min strategy the next fastest, and the strategies involving counting from 1 (sum and shortcut sum) the slowest.

Also as in previous studies, use of diverse strategies was evident within as well as between children. All eight children in the experiment used four of the five most common strategies on at least one trial; six of the eight used all five of them.

Although each child used a variety of strategies, individuals did vary considerably in their relative frequency of use of the different strategies. As can be seen in Table 3.4 four of the eight children used a single strategy on an absolute majority of trials. In two cases, this involved predominant use of the traditional sum strategy, in one it involved predominant use of the shortcut-sum approach, and in one case it involved predominant use of retrieval. The strategy use of the other four children did not show any single majority strategy; each of them used between three and six strategies on at least 10 trials each.

Strategy use changed substantially with pratice. Figure 3.1 illustrates the percent use of each strategy on the small-addend problems over five-session trial blocks. The first three blocks include performance on the first, second, and third groups of 35 problems that children encountered. The fourth block includes performance on the next 35 small-addend problems plus whatever additional small-addend

TABLE 3.4
Percent Use of Each Strategy by Each Child

Child	Sum	Retrieval	SCSum	Fing Rec	Min	Unknown	Guess	Count from First
Brittany	43	6	9	19	21	–	1	–
Christian	31	10	27	25	1	2	–	–
Danny	65	1	6	13	–	14	–	–
Jesse	0	23	68	1	2	4	–	–
Laine	69	5	1	6	1	–	17	–
Lauren	40	40	8	–	6	6	–	–
Ruth	13	42	9	8	17	1	2	6
Whitney	5	61	5	5	18	3	2	–
Total	34	22	17	11	9	4	2	1

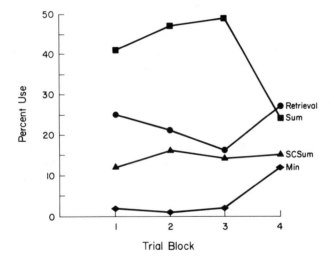

FIG. 3.1. Changes in frequency of strategy use over trial blocks.

problems that children encountered.[3] For most children, the fourth trial block roughly coincided with the period when large- as well as small-addend problems were presented (the last 4 weeks of the experiment).

---

[3]Although two children encountered enough additional small-addend problems to constitute an entire trial block, basing a group average for a fifth trial block on just their results would have led to a sample of children that was not comparable to the one that generated performance on the first four trial blocks.

As is evident in the figure, the greatest changes in strategy use on the small-addend problems occurred in trial block 4. The min strategy became much more common, retrieval became the single most frequent strategy, and use of the sum strategy was cut in half. Encountering the challenge problems and the other large-addend problems that were presented in the last 4 weeks of the experiment thus appeared to influence strategy use on small-addend problems as well as on large-addend ones.

Examination of individual children's performance suggested some degree of systematicity in the changes in strategy use. Children who initially most often guessed appeared to move toward frequent use of the sum strategy; those who initially most often used the sum strategy moved toward increasing use of the shortcut-sum, min, and retrieval approaches; those who initially most often used retrieval continued to use it most often. This, together with an a priori analysis of the strategies, suggested an ordering of strategies in which the progression from least to most advanced was guessing, the sum strategy, the shortcut-sum strategy, the min strategy, and retrieval. Each individual would always use a variety of strategies, but the trend would be toward more frequent use of the more advanced strategies.

Beyond this general trend toward more advanced strategies, we hypothesized that the particular changes in each child's performance would be toward more advanced strategies *that were nearby in the hypothesized ordering of the strategies.* That is, we hypothesized that individual children's strategy changes would be toward a somewhat more advanced strategy rather than toward a much more advanced one. One way to test this idea was to correlate each child's percentage of use of each strategy early in the experiment with that child's percentage of use of each strategy later in the experiment. If the hypothesized ordering of strategies was correct, and if changes were indeed toward increasing use of nearby rather than far away strategies, correlations between frequency of use of strategies hypothesized to be near each other (e.g., guessing and sum; min and retrieval) should be higher than correlations between frequency of strategies hypothesized to be more distant (e.g., guessing and min; sum and retrieval).

To test these hypotheses, we computed two sets of correlations. Each set of correlations related frequency of use of each of six strategies before presentation of the challenge problems to frequency of use of each of the six strategies during and after the challenge problems. Both analyses included the six most common approaches:

retrieval, the min strategy, shortcut-sum, finger recognition, sum, and guessing. One analysis involved correlations between earlier and later strategy use on small-addend problems. The other analysis involved correlations between early strategy use on small-addend problems (the only ones presented before the challenge problems) with later strategy use on large-addend problems. This latter correlation allowed examination of strategy transfer from small- to large-addend problems as well as stability and changes in strategy use over time.

First consider the analysis of earlier and later strategy use on the small-addend problems. One clear finding was that children who frequently used a strategy before the challenge problems also frequently used that strategy afterward. Early percent use of retrieval, the min strategy, the shortcut-sum strategy, and the sum strategy correlated $r = .57$, $r = .58$, $r = .59$, and $r = .61$ with later use of the same strategy (children never guessed on small-addend problems at time 2, so no correlation could be computed for guessing).

A second clear finding was an ordering of correlations in line with the hypothesized ordering of strategies. Among the 25 correlations between pairs of different strategies at the two times, 3 of the 4 most strongly positive correlations were between strategies that were adjacent in the hypothesized ordering of strategies. Percent use of guessing at time 1 correlated $r = .94$ with percent use of the sum strategy at time 2; percent finger recognition at time 1 correlated $r = .42$ with percent use of shortcut sum at time 2; percent min strategy use at time 1 correlated $r = .26$ with percent use of retrieval at time 2. In all cases, the direction of change involved time 1 use of the strategy hypothesized to be less advanced predicting time 2 use of the strategy hypothesized to be more advanced. Conversely, the most strongly negative of the 30 correlations was between the two strategies at the opposite ends of the scale. Percent use of guessing at time 1 correlated $r = -.74$ with percent use of retrieval at time 2. Because none of the children guessed on the small-addend problems at the end of the experiment, no correlation could be computed between percent retrieval at time 1 and percent guessing at time 2, which might have been expected to be even more strongly negatively related.

Similar relations were present in the correlations between percent use of each strategy on small-addend problems before the challenge problems and percent use of each strategy on large-addend problems during and after them. Children who used a strategy on the small-addend problems in the earlier part of the experiment continued to use that strategy later on the large-addend problems. Percent use of retrieval, the min strategy, the shortcut-sum strategy, the sum strategy, and guessing at time 1 correlated $r = .45$, $r = .66$, $r = .42$, $r = .70$, and $r = .99$ with percent use of the same strategy at time 2. Also, the three most strongly positive correlations between different strategies were between pairs of strategies hypothesized to be adjacent in the ordering. Percent finger recognition at time 1 and percent shortcut-sum use at time 2 correlated $r = .61$; percent guessing at time 1 and percent sum strategy use at time 2 correlated $r = .44$; percent retrieval at time 1 and percent min strategy use at time 2 correlated $r = .52$.

The correlation between percent retrieval at time 1 and percent min use at time 2 was especially interesting. Although it superficially seemed to represent movement from a more advanced to a less advanced strategy, it is important to remember that the retrievals at time 1 were on the small-addend problems and the min strategy uses at time 2 were on large-addend problems. Thus, children who most frequently used retrieval to solve the small-addend problems earlier in the experiment tended to use the min strategy when later confronted with the large-addend problems. Given that these preschoolers would have had a very hard time retrieving answers on large-addend problems such as $2 + 23$, it made sense that they would solve them by using the next most advanced approach that they knew, the min strategy.

These correlations do not indicate that children progressed through a simple sequence of strategies, in which each strategy replaced its predecessor. The reality was far more complex than this. Individual children used more and less advanced strategies at all times. Nonetheless, the data did indicate that amidst the diversity, there was also a degree of consistency in the changes in children's strategy use. They moved toward increasing use of strategies that were somewhat, but not greatly, more advanced relative to the ones they used initially.

Discovery of the Min Strategy

Especially important for our goal of examining strategy construction, most children discovered the min strategy. We set two criteria for saying when a given child made the discovery. To meet the *strict criterion,* children needed to unambiguously count from the larger addend and to accurately describe the way in which they had counted. To meet the *loose criterion,* children needed either to count from the larger addend but be unable to accurately describe the counting or to use an approach that combined characteristics of the min strategy with those of other strategies. Thus, a girl who could be heard on the videotape counting from 4 on 2 + 4, but who said that she had counted from one, would meet the loose criterion but not the strict one. To meet the strict criterion, she would have to say that she counted from 4. In the course of the experiment, seven of the eight children met the loose criterion, and six of the eight met the strict one. Meeting the strict criterion proved to be an important event not only for indicating awareness of having used the new strategy but also for predicting subsequent generalization of the strategy to other problems.

The Quality of Discovery. One of the advantages of the present trial-by-trial approach to strategy construction was that it yielded a qualitative sense of the discovery process, as well as numerous quantitative measures. Following are a pair of protocols of Lauren solving addition problems. The first represents the trial on which Lauren first met the loose criterion for using the min strategy; this trial occurred in her fifth session.

E: *How much is 5 + 2?*

L: Puts up five fingers on one hand and two on the other, counts three fingers on the hand with five fingers up, stops, pauses, says '7' as if unsure.

E: *Seven, OK, how did you know that?*

L: *Cause I thought . . . Cause I thought in my head.*

E: *OK, can you tell me what you thought in your head?*

L: *I thought if there's 5 and there's 2 more, then that's 7, cause if 5 and 1 is 6, then 5 and 2 are 7."*

As suggested by this example, on trials that met the loose but not the strict criterion, it often was difficult to cleanly separate the min strategy from solution by analogy to other problems. For example, in the case just cited, it was unclear whether Lauren actually used the min strategy to count on from 5 or whether she analogized from the related problem 5 + 1. We were willing to conclude that her performance met the loose criterion for using the min strategy, because even the analogical interpretation implies that she counted on (or did the equivalent operation of adding one) to the known answer (6) to obtain the new answer (7). Thus, at minimum, Lauren had counted on from a number larger than one, the largest innovation embodied by the min strategy.

All ambiguity was gone when 10 sessions later, Lauren met the strict criterion.

E: *How much is 6 + 3?*

L: (Long pause) *Nine.*

E: *OK, how did you know that?*

L: *I think I said . . . I think I said . . . oops, um . . . I think he said . . . 8 was 1 and . . . um . . . I mean 7 was 1, 8 was 2, 9 was 3.*

E: *OK.*

L: *Six and three are nine.*

E: *How did you know to do that? Why didn't you count '1, 2, 3, 4, 5, 6, 7, 8, 9'? How come you did '6, 7, 8, 9'?*

L: *Cause then you have to count all those numbers.*

E: *OK, well how did you know you didn't have to count all of those numbers?*

L: *Why didn't . . . well I don't have to if I don't want to.*

For purposes of analysis, we dichotomized children's strategy discoveries as meeting either the strict or the loose criterion. Actually, however, the degree to which the discovery processes reflected understanding and insight fell along a continuum. At one extreme, the most insightful explanations reflected understanding not only that a new strategy had been used but why the new strategy was a good idea. For example, one child explained why she had counted from 4 on 4 + 3 by saying that "I don't have to count a very long ways if I start from 4, I just have to do 3 more"). At the other extreme, some children insisted that they had retrieved the answer, and gave no evidence that they recognized that they had counted from the larger addend. In between were children who initially denied that they had done anything unusual, but when probed indicated some awareness of counting from the larger addend. In the next chapter, we examine a number of protocols that illustrate the range of degrees of insight that accompanied children's first use of the new strategy.

Problems on Which Discoveries Occurred. The particular problems on which children first appeared to use the min strategy were quite diverse. Of the seven children who discovered the strategy, only two did so on the same problem (4 + 3). The specific problems on which the children first used the min strategy were 2 + 5, 4 + 1, 3 + 9, 1 + 24, 5 + 2, and 4 + 3. These problems did not deviate from the characteristics of the overall set in any notable way.

Solution Times on Discovery Trials. Solution times were longer than usual on the trials on which children discovered the min strategy. This was most evident in median solution time. The median RT on the seven discovery trials was 17.8 sec, whereas the overall median RT was 9.4 sec. Mean RT was also somewhat longer on the discovery trials, 16.2 vs 12.8 sec. The differences were larger if discovery is equated with first use of the min strategy to the strict criterion. Here, both median and mean RT's were twice as great on the 6 discovery trials as on trials in general (22.6 vs 9.4 and 25.7 vs 12.8 sec. respectively).

The difference cannot be explained on the basis of the problems on which the discovery occurred being particularly difficult. Five of the seven problems on which the discoveries were made (71%) were small-addend problems, almost identical to the 72% for the set as a whole. Pauses, false starts, and slow counting all seemed to contribute to the length of time children required on the trial where they first used the new strategy.

Changes Leading up to Discovery
of the Min Strategy

The Time Course of Discovery. Children differed greatly in how long they took to discover the min strategy. As shown in Fig. 3.2, the first child to discover the strategy did so in her second session. At the other extreme, one child never discovered the strategy in his 23 sessions and another first used it in the last of her 22 sessions. In terms of number of days from the beginning of the experiment to the discovery, the first discovery came 2 days after the experiment started; the last discovery came 73 days after the experiment started.

It was not always the case that children met the loose criterion before meeting the strict criterion. Four of the six children who ever met the strict criterion met it on the first trial on which they gave any evidence of using the min strategy. It also was not the case that children consistently met the loose criterion earlier in the experiment than the strict criterion. The mean number of sessions prior to meeting the loose criterion was 13; the mean number of sessions prior to

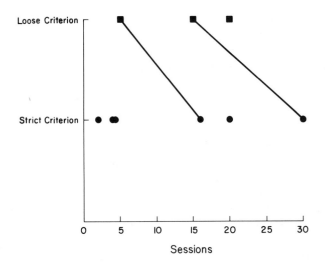

FIG. 3.2. Session in which each child first used the min strategy. Lines connecting dots for loose and strict criteria uses indicate when a given child first used the strategy to each criterion.

meeting the strict criterion was 14. Similarly, the mean number of days prior to meeting the loose criterion was 37; the mean number of days prior to meeting the strict criterion was 35. As shown in Fig. 3.2, some children met the strict criterion quite early in the experiment; others did not meet even the loose criterion until quite late.

Changes in Solution Times. The longer solution times that characterized the trials on which children discovered the min strategy also characterized the trials just before the discovery occurred. This could be seen in the performance of the five children who first used the min strategy on some trial other than the first trial of a session. Recall that the overall mean and median RTs were 13 and 9 sec, respectively. On the trial immediately before each child's discovery, the mean time was 25 sec, and the median time was 18 sec. On the trial before each child met the strict criterion, the mean RT was 33 sec and the median RT 18 sec. A similar picture emerged for all trials before the discovery but within the same session. On these 20 trials, the mean RT was 18 sec and the median RT was 14 sec.

What did these relatively long solution times reflect? One possibility was that both they and the subsequent discovery of the min strategy were due to the preceding problems being difficult ones. This was not the case, however; 14 of the 16 problems preceding the discoveries but within the same session were small-addend problems. In comparative terms, 88% of the problems encountered in the session of discovery prior to the trial of discovery were small-addend problems, versus 72% for the practice set as a whole.

Another possibility was that inability to solve the immediately preceding problems caused both the long solution times and the subsequent discovery of the min strategy. Again, however, the data provided little support for this interpretation. Prior to discovering the min strategy, children had answered correctly 12 of the 16 problems that they had encountered within the session. This level of accuracy, 75%, was not substantially worse than the 85% correct answers that children generated across the entire practice set. Further, three of the four errors were generated by a single child; the other four children collectively made only one error on the 12 trials they encountered in the same session but before their discoveries. This, together with the fact that two other children used the min strategy for the first time on the first trial of a session, indicated that incorrect answers are not necessary to motivate discovery of a new strategy. However, the long solution times just prior to the discoveries do suggest a heightening of cognitive activity even without incorrect answers to motivate it.

The Role of Counting From the First Addend. Several previous theoretical accounts of the development of the min strategy suggested that counting from the first addend mediates the transition from use of the sum to use of the min strategy (Neches, 1987; Resnick & Neches, 1984; Secada, Fuson, & Hall, 1983). This view was based on a rational analysis of differences between the sum and min strategies, and on previous observations that children sometimes counted from the first addend even when it was the smaller of the two addends. Our method of examining strategy use on each trial allowed a more rigorous test of the link between counting from the first addend and discovery of the min strategy.

The data provided little support for the hypothesized link between the two strategies. Only one of the eight children in the experiment ever counted from the first addend on trials where it was the smaller addend. This child did discover the count-from-first strategy in the same session in which she first used the min strategy, which might be interpreted as support for the hypothesized linkage. However, she used it after, rather than before, her discovery of the min approach. Moreover, six other children discovered the min strategy without ever having used the count-from-first strategy.

These results regarding the count-from-first strategy have at least two implications. First, the fact that only one of the eight children gave any evidence of using it, and then only on seven trials, makes clear why some investigators have reported that children use it and others have not. Simply put, the strategy is used, but only occasionally. Second, the fact that most children never used the count-from-first approach but did discover the min strategy indicated that discovery of the min strategy cannot generally be based on prior use of the count-from-first strategy, as suggested by Neches' (1987) model.

The Role of the Shortcut-Sum Strategy. The shortcut-sum strategy appeared to represent a much better candidate as a mediator of discovery of the min strategy. It was used by a higher percentage of children — seven of the eight, as opposed to one of the eight. It was used on many more trials — 230, as opposed to 7. As might be expected in a transitional strategy, most children used it on some but not a huge number of trials. Of the seven children who ever used the strategy, five used it on between 5% and 9% of trials. The other two used it considerably more often; it was one child's most frequent strategy (68% of trials) and another child's second most frequent (27%).

Discovery of the shortcut-sum strategy was related both empirically and conceptually to discovery of the min strategy. Empirically, five of the seven children who discovered the min strategy had recently discovered the shortcut-sum strategy: two first used it two sessions before their first use of the min strategy, one first used it one session before, and two first used it in the same session on an earlier trial. This does not mean that discovery of the shortcut-sum approach was invariably followed by rapid discovery of the min strategy. The child who used the shortcut-sum strategy the most often (140 trials) did not discover the min strategy until 20 sessions after he started using the shortcut-sum approach, and the one child who never discovered the min strategy had occasionally used the shortcut-sum approach over his previous 22 sessions. Nor does it mean that use of the shortcut-sum strategy was necessary for use of the min strategy. One of the eight children discovered the min strategy without any apparent prior use of the shortcut-sum approach. Overall, however, discovery of the shortcut-sum approach made it likely that discovery of the min strategy would follow soon after.

Another reason for thinking that the shortcut-sum strategy was related to discovery of the min strategy was the opportunity that experience with it gave for learning the advantages of reversing the order of the addends. On all strategies other than shortcut sum, children were equally accurate (within 5% of the same percent correct) regardless of whether the first or second addend was larger. In contrast, when children used the shortcut-sum approach, they were considerably more accurate on problems where the first addend was larger than on ones where the second addend was (92% vs. 72% correct).

This difference makes sense when we think about the demands of executing the shortcut-sum strategy. When children count from one to the number that corresponds to the first addend, they just need to monitor their counting to see if the running sum matches the addend that they are counting; when it does, that counting operation is complete. In contrast, starting at this point and counting beyond it by the number of counts indicated by the other addend requires keeping track of the running total count as well as of whether the number of counts representing the second addend has reached the target of the second addend's size. Because of the greater memory demand of this second counting operation, the difficulty of correctly executing the shortcut-sum strategy would seem likely to go up sharply with the size of whichever addend is counted second. Therefore, it is advantageous to keep as small as possible the size of the addend that is counted second and to reverse the order of the addends if that will place the smaller addend second.

There was also empirical evidence that children sometimes reversed the order of the addends when executing the shortcut-sum strategy. The evidence involved children's pause times. On some trials, children detectably paused at points corresponding to one of the addends. The pauses on such trials indicated that six of the seven children who used the shortcut-sum approach sometimes executed it by reversing the order of the addends. For example, rather than solving 2 + 5 by counting "1, 2 . . . 3, 4, 5, 6, 7", they solved it by counting "1, 2, 3, 4, 5 . . . 6, 7." This is not intended to imply that children necessarily first learned that they could reverse addend order on shortcut-sum trials. A number of them had previously reversed addend order on sum strategy trials (see also Baroody, 1984). However, the greater accuracy of the shortcut-sum approach when the first addend was larger may have provided specific evidence of the potential usefulness of reversing the addends on other problems so that the longer count could be executed under the easier conditions.

The general nature of the shortcut-sum strategy also made it a plausible transitional approach. As previously noted, it is like the sum strategy, and unlike the min strategy, in that it involves counting from one and naming each number word from one through the sum. On the other hand, it is like the min strategy, and unlike the sum strategy, in that numbers are not repeated twice and in that counting of one of the addends proceeds from a point greater than one. Together, these conceptual and empirical considerations make it likely that acquisition of the shortcut-sum strategy is often transitional to discovery of the min strategy.

Predictors of Strategy Discovery. Two multiple regression analyses were performed to determine which, if any, aspects of children's pretest performance were related to the number of sessions they required to discover the min strategy. One analysis examined predictors of the session of first use of the min strategy by the loose or the strict criterion, whichever came first. The other examined predictors of the session of first use of the strategy by the strict criterion. The predictors within each analysis were number of problems correct on the magnitude comparison task, number of problems correct on the three counting-of-objects tasks, time per count on the free counting task, percent correct on the addition pretest, and percent of answers correctly retrieved on the addition pretest. Age, grade, sex, and total number of problems that each child received in the practice phase of the experiment were also included as predictor variables.[4]

None of the measures of knowledge prior to the experiment was significantly related to the session at which children first used the min strategy to at least the loose criterion. The correlations ranged from $r = .39$ to $r = -.34$. The only variable tested that was significantly related to this outcome was sex. Girls discovered the min strategy significantly earlier than did boys $r = .68$, $df = 7$, $p < .05$.

In the parallel analysis of first use of the min strategy to the strict criterion, none of the variables proved to be significant predictors. Sex of the child again was the best predictor, $r = .58$, with girls discovering the min strategy to the strict criterion earlier than boys did. Again, none of the measures of pre-experimental knowledge of addition, magnitude comparison, or counting correlated even $r = .50$ with subsequent discovery of the min strategy to this criterion.

---

[4]One child did not discover the min strategy and two children did not discover it to the strict criterion. Within each analysis, the session of discovery of children who did not meet the relevant discovery criterion was arbitrarily set to the session immediately following the last session in which any child made the discovery to that criterion.

Thus, pretest knowledge of addition and related skills did not prove to be a very good predictor of the children's order of discovery of the min strategy. This may have been due to the range of children's knowledge being somewhat restricted, with all but one child having quite good knowledge, or may indicate that children highest in knowledge are not necessarily the first to discover new strategies.

Strategy Generalization

In this experiment, we focused not only on how children discovered the min strategy but also on how they generalized it to other problems once they had made the initial discovery. The data of three of the eight children were not very useful with regard to this question. One child did not discover the strategy. Two others discovered it in the last week of the experiment, so that there were few trials on which they could have generalized the new strategy to new problems. However, the data of the other five children allowed us to examine how children generalized the min strategy once they discovered it.

Initial Level of Generalization. Most children rarely used the min strategy in the period immediately after they discovered it. This was not simply due to children being able to retrieve answers by the time they discovered the min strategy and therefore having little incentive to use the min approach. Even when compared to the two other counting approaches, the sum and shortcut-sum strategies, the min approach still was not used very often in this initial period. In the first five sessions after children discovered the min strategy, they used the strategy on only 12% of trials on which they used any of the three counting strategies.

Effects of Challenge Problems. As shown in Fig. 3.3, the picture changed dramatically when the challenge problems were introduced. When children were confronted with problems such as 23 + 2, which were easy to solve by the min strategy but very difficult via the other two counting approaches, they began to use the min strategy much more often. Their use of the min strategy, which had been below 20% of trials on which they counted, jumped to more than 60% of such trials. Further, the gains continued in the last 3 weeks of the experiment, when varied problems were presented.

The picture remained basically the same when comparisons were limited to the small-addend problems that were given both before and

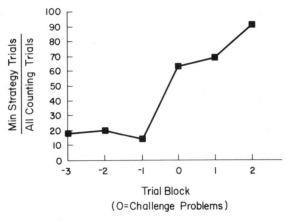

FIG. 3.3. Min strategy use before and after challenge problems.

after the challenge problems. We examined percent use of the min strategy of the five children who ever used the min strategy on these small addend problems. In the three trial blocks prior to the challenge problems, percent use of the min strategy on these problems was 10%, 12% and 11% respectively. Following the challenge problems, however, they used the min strategy on 45% of trials on such problems. Four of the five individual children used the min strategy more often on the small-addend problems after the challenge set than they had on any of the trial blocks prior to the challenge problems (the fifth child used the min strategy once on a small-addend problem before the challenge problems and not at all on them after the challenge problems).

Effects of Conscious Discovery on Subsequent Generalization. As previously noted, children varied greatly in the degree of insight that accompanied their strategy discovery process. For purposes of analysis, we divided children into the six who met the strict criterion, and thus were aware that they had counted from the larger addend, and the three who met only the loose criterion, and thus did not seem aware of doing so.[5]

---

[5]Two children, Lauren and Christian first used the min strategy without any clear awareness and later used it with awareness. Their trials after the initial use but prior to the conscious discovery were classified with those of the "discovery without awareness"

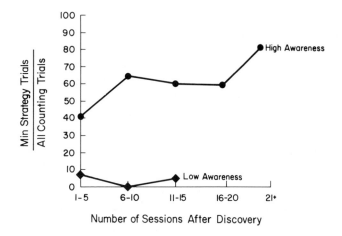

FIG. 3.4. Min strategy use following discovery with high and low awareness.

As shown in Fig. 3.4, there were large differences in the degree of generalization of the min strategy as a function of whether children showed awareness that they had counted from the larger addend. Children who showed such awareness used the min strategy more often relative to other counting strategies from the time of discovery. Over time, the min strategy became the dominant counting strategy for these children. In contrast, children who could be seen and/or heard counting from the larger addend, but who appeared unaware that they had done so, showed very little generalization of the strategy. They used it on fewer than 10% of trials on which they used a counting strategy.

Predictors of Generalization. A parallel analysis to the one aimed at determining predictors of when children discovered the min strategy was conducted to examine predictors of how often they used the strategy once they discovered it. None of the pretest measures was closely related to subsequent number of uses of the min strategy. The correlations ranged from $r = .09$ to $r = -.25$. The relation between total number of trials and total uses of the min strategy also was only $r = .40$. This was a surprisingly weak relation given the wide range in

---

group. Their trials following the conscious discovery were classified with those of the "discovery with awareness group."

the number of problems children encountered, 130–244. Combined with the much stronger relation of encountering the challenge problems to frequency of use of the min strategy, the finding suggested that the types of problems children encountered had a greater influence on their generalization of the min strategy than did the number of problems they encountered.

CONCLUSIONS

A number of findings emerged from the strategy-discovery experiment. Most 4- and 5-year-olds were able to discover the min strategy. Some discovered it to the strict criterion, by illustrating awareness of counting from the larger addend. Others (sometimes the same child earlier in the experiment) met only the loose criterion, in which the child appeared to use the min strategy but did not seem clearly aware of using a new approach. The discovery tended to be accompanied by unusually long solution times, both on the trial of discovery and on the immediately preceding trials within the same session.

Counting from the first addend did not mediate most children's acquisition of the min strategy. However, the shortcut-sum strategy did seem to be a common transitional approach. Awareness of using a new strategy was strongly related to subsequent generalization of the strategy, as was exposure to the challenge problems that were very difficult to solve by use of existing strategies but quite easy to solve by use of the min strategy.

As clear as these general patterns, however, was the child-to-child variability in the strategy construction process. Length of time to discover the strategy, amount of use once the strategy was discovered, reactions to the challenge problems, and the quality of the discovery experience all varied tremendously. It seemed that the best way to examine this variability was to examine individual children's strategy construction processes. The experiences of five children are examined in the next chapter.

4

Case Studies

Just as children use diverse approaches to solve problems, they also use diverse approaches to construct new strategies. The extensive data on each child's performance that were yielded by the present study made these individual differences in strategy construction impossible to ignore.

Case studies provided a way of capturing the variability in the strategy construction process. They allowed us to follow an individual's progress from the beginning of the pretest to the end of the practice phase. They also allowed us to consider simultaneously the changes that occurred in diverse aspects of the child's performance. Further, they provided a context within which to compare each child's discovery and generalization of the new strategy to those of other children.

In this chapter, we examine the experiences of five of the eight children who participated in the experiment: Brittany, Lauren, Whitney, Christian, and Ruth. They were chosen because they were the five who discovered the min strategy early enough that it was possible to observe their generalization of the strategy to new problems. The other three children either did not discover the min strategy or discovered it in the last week of the study. Because our primary interest was in the discovery and generalization processes, we decided to focus on those children whose performance provided the greatest amount of relevant data about these processes.

The case studies complement the data presented in the previous chapter by providing a qualitative sense of what strategy construction is like. Children's own words as they first generate and attempt to describe a new strategy convey a feel for the process that quantitative measures cannot duplicate. When viewed in the context of ongoing changes in quantifiable dimensions of the child's performance, the protocols become even more meaningful. Here we present the five case studies starting with Brittany, a child who at the outset was not especially knowledgeable about arithmetic, but who eventually generalized the min strategy the most widely of any of the children.

BRITTANY

When the experiment began, Brittany was 4-years 9 months old, the third youngest of the eight children in the study. Her knowledge of arithmetic started out at a relatively low level. On the pretest, she had the second lowest percent correct, 65%, of the eight children. Her median solution time on the pretest addition problems, 13.6 sec, was the second slowest. She was one of two children who did not correctly retrieve any of the answers.

During the 11 weeks of the practice phase, Brittany's performance improved considerably. She correctly answered 87% of the small-addend problems, considerably above her 65% correct on these problems on the pretest and within 2% of the group average. Her median RT was 9.6 sec, again considerably better than her median pretest time and within a second of the group average. She dealt especially effectively with the large-addend problems presented in the last 4 weeks of the experiment. Her 90% correct on these problems made her the second most accurate on them among the eight children. Further, she was one of two children who were actually slightly more accurate on large-addend than on small-addend problems. Thus, although Brittany started out as one of the least skillful adders, she became one of the more skillful, particularly on the large problems.

One source of the changes in Brittany's speed and accuracy involved changes in her strategy use. As shown in Fig. 4.1, she started out using the sum strategy on the large majority of trials. In her 12th session, she discovered the min strategy to the strict criterion.

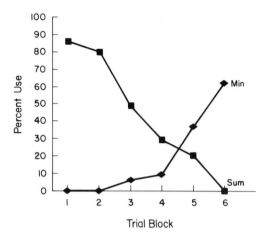

FIG. 4.1. Strategy use over trial blocks for Brittany.

Thereafter, she used the min strategy on a large and increasing percentage of trials on which she counted. This enabled her to deal effectively with large-addend problems such as 22 + 3, which were difficult for many of the other children.

Brittany was one of the two children who first used the shortcut-sum strategy in the same session in which she first used the min approach. Her initial use of the shortcut-sum strategy was on the first trial of the session, on the problem 2 + 1. The trial proceeded as follows:

E: *How much is 2 + 1?*

B: *One* (puts out finger on one hand), *two* (puts out a second finger on the same hand, then puts out a third finger on the other hand) *Oh that's easy, that's three.*

E: *How did you know that?*

B: *I never counted.*

E: *You just knew it?*

B: *I knew it . . . I just blobbed around*

As is seen later, Brittany was not the only child who denied counting in her initial use of a strategy even though she could be heard counting on the trial.

Brittany again used the shortcut-sum approach on the second problem of the session, 5 + 1. On the third problem, 4 + 1, she put up her fingers and recognized that there were five. On all three of these problems, her answers were fast as well as accurate; the three RTs ranged from 4 to 6 sec.

On the fourth trial of the session, Brittany discovered the min strategy.

E: *OK Brittany, how much is 2 + 5?*
B: *2 + 5 —* (whispers) *6, 7 — it's 7.*
E: *How did you know that?*
B: (excitedly) *Never counted.*
E: *You didn't count?*
B: *Just said it — I just said after six something — seven — six, seven.*
E: *You did? Why did you say 6, 7?*
B: *Cause I wanted to see what it really was.*
E: *OK, well — so, did you — what — you didn't have to count at one, you didn't count 1,2,3, you just said 6,7?*
B: *Yeah — smart answer.*

Brittany's discovery of the min strategy was like that of many of the other children in that it occurred in close proximity to her discovery of the shortcut-sum approach. However, her solution times were atypical. Both her RT on the trial where she discovered the min strategy (5.7 sec) and the prior times in the same session were much faster than those of any of the other children in the session where they first met the strict criterion for using the min strategy.

Although Brittany seemed excited by her initial use of the min strategy and explicitly recognized that she had given a "smart answer," she did not immediately begin to use the new approach very often. In the remainder of the session and in the following three sessions, she used the standard sum strategy 16 times but never used either the min or the shortcut-sum strategy. Then, in the fourth session following her discovery of the min and shortcut-sum strategies, Brittany used the two new strategies on all seven trials. She used the shortcut-sum approach six times and the min strategy once. This might have been expected to signal a permanent change in her strategy use, but it did not. In the next eight sessions, Brittany used the min strategy on only six trials and the shortcut-sum on only one (as opposed to 15 uses of the sum strategy).

The situation changed dramatically with presentation of the challenge problems. On the seven challenge problems that Brittany received, she used the shortcut-sum three times and the min strategy three times. In the first session after the challenge set, she used the shortcut-sum approach on three of seven trials. In the session after that, she used the shortcut-sum on two of seven trials and the min strategy on four of seven. Following this, the min strategy became her dominant approach. In the seven remaining sessions, she used the min strategy on 36 trials, the shortcut-sum strategy on four, and the standard sum strategy on only one. The changes in use of the min strategy that occurred during and after presentation of the challenge problems are illustrated in Fig. 4.2 for Brittany and for the other children in the experiment.

Brittany was like a number of children in that her use of the min strategy increased considerably during and after presentation of the challenge problems. She was unusual, however, in the extent of the change and in her frequent use of the min strategy even on small-addend problems where many of the other children retrieved answers. After the challenge problems, she used the min strategy on 14 of the 23 small-addend problems that she encountered (61%). By the end of

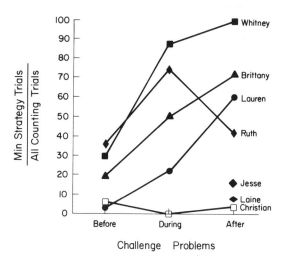

FIG. 4.2. Percent min strategy use relative to other counting strategies before, during, and after challenge problems.

the study, she had used the min strategy on a higher percentage of trials than any of the other children.

LAUREN

When the experiment began, Lauren was a 63-month-old member of the pre-kindergarten class. Despite her being in the pre-kindergarten class, her pretest performance was in many ways the most advanced of any of the children. She was the only child who answered all problems correctly. She had the second highest percent of answers that were both retrieved and correct (35%). Her median RT was the fourth fastest of the children in the study (7.5 sec).

Lauren maintained her high degree of accuracy in the practice phase of the experiment. Her 98% correct in the practice phase was the highest of any of the children. Her accuracy on small-addend problems (100%) and on large-addend ones (94%) were both the highest for that subcategory of problems. Surprisingly, however, her fairly fast solution times on the pretest gave way to considerably slower times in the practice phase. Her median RT on all problems, 11.4 sec, was the slowest of the eight children in the experiment. Further, her speed declined in absolute as well as relative terms. On the small-addend problems, which were presented both in the pretest and throughout the practice phase, Lauren's median RT slowed from 7.5 sec. on the pretest to 10.3 sec in the practice phase.

These slower times were paralleled by changes in her strategy use. Over the first 15 sessions of the practice phase (the ones prior to the challenge problems), Lauren moved toward more use of the time-consuming sum strategy and less use of retrieval. As shown in Fig. 4.3, by the third trial block, Lauren was using retrieval on only 10% of small-addend problems. On the pretest, she had retrieved answers to 35% of these same problems (all correctly).

Lauren's strategy use again changed when she encountered the challenge problems. Where she previously had been using retrieval on a small and decreasing percentage of trials, she now began using it on almost all of the small-addend problems. She used retrieval on 21 of the 24 small-addend problems that followed presentation of the challenge problems (vs. 4 of 35 in the trial block immediately before). Conversely, she used the sum strategy on only 2 of 24 small-addend problems following the challenge set, versus 30 of 35 in the trial block before.

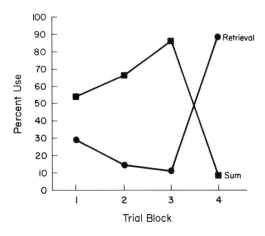

FIG. 4.3. Strategy use over trial blocks for Lauren.

Lauren's initial uses of the shortcut-sum and min strategies occurred fairly close together. She first used the shortcut-sum strategy in the third session. She used it three times in that session, and once in the following session. The session after that (her fifth session) was when she discovered the min strategy to the loose criterion. On the first trial of the session, Lauren used the sum strategy to solve 4 + 3; on the second trial, she used the shortcut-sum strategy to solve 2 + 1; on the third trial, she used the min strategy to solve 5 + 2. The full protocol of this trial was presented in chapter 3; basically, Lauren said that 5 and 2 was 7, because since 5 and 1 was 6, then 5 and 2 was 7.

In the next session, Lauren used the shortcut-sum strategy once and did not use the min strategy at all. In the session after that, she used the shortcut-sum strategy twice and the min strategy once. Again, her use of the min strategy met the loose but not the strict criterion. In the following eight sessions, both strategies virtually disappeared. She used the shortcut-sum strategy on only 2 of the 56 trials and did not use the min strategy at all.

This trend ended when Lauren encountered the challenge problems. On the first day, Lauren used the shortcut-sum strategy on five of seven problems. Her solution times were quite long (median RT = 19 sec), as would be expected from the amount of counting needed to solve these problems. In this session, she solved all seven problems correctly, which was quite unusual for these difficult problems.

The second set of challenge problems elicited Lauren's first use of the min strategy to the strict criterion. Her behavior leading up to the discovery was intriguing. The following is the protocol for the first two trials of the session.

E: *Lauren, how much is 23 + 2?*

L: (rapidly moves her fingers back and fourth) *50.*

E: *50, ok, and how did you know that?*

L: *Cause, I counted in my head.*

E: *Can you tell me how you counted in your head?*

L: *1, 2, 3, 4, 5, 6, 7, 8, 9, 10, 11, 12, 13, 14, 15, 16, 17, 18, 19, 20, 21, 22, 23, 24, 25* (pauses and smiles)

E: *What's wrong?*

L: *Nothing.*

E: *What's the answer, what was the answer to 23 + 2? You said 40* (sic) *is that right?*

L: *I mean 25. I forgot.*

E: *25?*

L: *Oh well.*

E: *Let's try another one Lauren. How much is 12 + 4?*

L: (long pause) *16?*

E: *How did you know that?*

L: *Cause I counted in my head.*

E: *Can you tell me how you counted in your head . . . ?*

L: *Uh, 1, 2, 3, 4, 5, 6, 7, 8, 9, 10, 11, 12* (pats table with hand) *13* (pats table with hand) *14* (pats table) *15* (pats table) *16* (pats table), *17, 18, 19, 20, 21* (some pats mixed in with these counts, but not clearly related.) *Oops.*

E: *The answer was . . . it was 12 + 4, that's 16 right? You said it was 16.*

L: *I know but I counted that way though.*

On the next two problems, 7 + 2 and 22 + 4, Lauren said that she retrieved the answer. However, her very long solution times on the two problems, 29 and 68 sec, together with the likely unfamiliarity of at least the second problem, cast doubt on this explanation. Lauren had generated comparably long solution times on the first two trials where she said she used the shortcut sum approach, 41 and 53 sec, respectively. Although our classification rule led us to classify the first two as shortcut-sum trials and the next two as retrieval trials, it seemed likely that she used the shortcut-sum strategy on all four.

The next trial elicited Lauren's first use of the min strategy to the strict criterion. As illustrated in the protocol in chapter 3, Lauren said that on this problem, 6 + 3, she counted by saying "7 was 1, 8 was 2, 9 was 3." She also explained that this was a better idea than counting from 1, "cause then you don't have to count all those numbers." Lauren also used the min strategy on one of the three remaining problems in the session (24 + 3). On the other two, 13 + 2 and 3 + 7, she said that the answer "just popped into my head."

In the nine sessions after the challenge set, Lauren used retrieval on most of the small-addend problems and used mainly retrieval and the min strategy on the large-addend problems. The prominence of the min strategy substantially increased over that which it had enjoyed before the challenge problems. Prior to that time, Lauren used the min approach on fewer than 10% of trials on which she used one of the three counting strategies. After it, she used the min strategy on 70% of such trials. Thus, the min strategy replaced the sum strategy as Lauren's most common approach to problems where she could not retrieve the answer.

WHITNEY

At the beginning of the study, Whitney was a 52-month-old pre-kindergartener, the youngest child in the experiment. She was ill several times during the course of the practice phase and therefore received fewer practice problems than any other child in the study. Despite her youth and relative lack of practice, however, she was one of the first children to meet the strong criterion for discovery of the min strategy. Moreover, she used it on the second highest percentage of trials of any of the children in the study.

On the pretest, Whitney had the second shortest median RT (6.5 sec), and also the second highest percentage of retrieval (55%). However, she was only the fifth most accurate of the eight children, answering 70% of problems correctly.

During the practice phase, Whitney maintained both her frequent use of retrieval and her not especially accurate performance. Her percent retrieval in the practice phase, 61%, was the highest of any of the children, far higher than the next highest child's percentage (42%). However, she never became very accurate. Her 78% correct in the practice phase was the second least accurate of the eight children. Her accuracy was relatively low on both retrieval and nonretrieval trials.

Whitney's high percentage of use of retrieval and relatively low accuracy when she reported doing so raised questions about the accuracy of the assessments of her strategies. However, the types of problems on which she was classified as using various strategies, and her pattern of accuracies on them, suggested that the assessments were accurate. In particular, she was classified as using retrieval on 94% of items with smaller addends of 1, 63% of items with smaller addends of 2, 27% with smaller addends of 3, and 29% with smaller addends of 4. Also lending credence to the strategy assessments, when she was classified as using the min strategy, she was correct on 100% of problems with smaller addends of 1 or 2, 64% of problems with smaller addends of 3, and 0% of problems with smaller addends of 4.

Although Whitney used retrieval on a high percentage of trials throughout the experiment, the relative frequency with which she used the three counting strategies underwent substantial change. In the pretest and in the first session of the practice phase, Whitney used the sum strategy four times and never used either the shortcut-sum or the min strategy. She first used the shortcut-sum strategy in the second practice session, on the problem 3 + 5. It never became one of her favorite approaches, though. She used it on only 6 of 130 practice phase trials. Following her initial use of the shortcut-sum approach, she did not use it at all for the next seven sessions.

Whitney's first use of the min strategy came in her fourth session. She had been correct on all three trials in the session up to the point at which she first used the min approach. On the first two trials, she quickly retrieved the answers to 4 + 2 and 1 + 4. On the third trial, she used the sum strategy to solve 5 + 3. Her RT on this trial was exceptionally long though, 56 sec. Thus, Whitney, like Lauren, took much more than the usual amount of time to solve the problem immediately before her discovery of the min strategy, despite having answered correctly all previous problems in the session.

On the trial on which Whitney first used the min strategy, her RT was also very long, 28 sec. Her description of her performance on this trial was like Brittany's, in that she audibly counted, but acknowledged counting from a number greater than one only after denying that she had done any counting.

E: *How much is 4 + 3?*
W: (mumble) *6, 7, I think it's 7.*

E: *Seven, ok, how did you know that?*

W: *Because I'm smart and I just knew it.*

E: *Can you tell me, I heard you counting. I heard you. Tell me how you counted.*

W: *I just — I didn't count anything . . . I just added numbers onto it.*

E: *Can you tell me how you added numbers?*

W: *No.*

E: *Come on Whitney — come on, we have to do this, OK?*

W: *OK, 3, add one makes 4, add one more makes 5, add one more makes 6, add one more makes 7, add one more makes 8.*

E: *Wait, but how did you know what 4 + 3 was?*

W: *Cause I did what I just showed you. I just used my mouth to figure it out.*

Although Whitney said that she counted from 3, the videotape of her performance made it more likely that she counted from 5. The initial mumbled sound was clearly a single word, and sounded most like 5. On subsequent counts where all of the counting could be heard clearly, Whitney consistently counted from the larger addend, though often denying that she had counted at all. Therefore, we concluded that her counting on this trial was "5,6,7."

As with both Brittany and Lauren, Whitney's initial discovery did not quickly lead to much use of the min strategy. In the seven sessions that followed her discovery and that preceded presentation of the challenge problems, Whitney used the min strategy on only 2 of 49 trials.

When the challenge problems were presented, however, Whitney, again like Lauren and Brittany, substantially increased her use of the min strategy. On the eight challenge problems that she encountered, she used the min approach seven times. The only problem on which she did not use it was the one with the smallest addends, 7 + 2.

In her seven sessions following the challenge problems, Whitney, once again like Lauren and Brittany, continued to use the min strategy more often, and the sum and shortcut-sum strategies less often, then she had before. Before the challenge problems, she had used the sum strategy on five trials, the shortcut-sum strategy on four trials, and the min strategy on three. After the challenge problems, she used the min strategy on 14 trials, the shortcut-sum strategy on 2 trials, and the sum strategy on none.

Like Lauren, and unlike Brittany, Whitney's use of the min strategy following the challenge problems was concentrated on the large-addend problems. Even on the small-addend problems, however, she increased her percentage of use of the min strategy relative to the other counting strategies. From the time when she first used the min strategy to the time when she encountered the challenge problems, Whitney used the min strategy on only 4% of problems. She used it on 22% of the small-addend problems that were presented after the challenge set. The difference suggests that Whitney's experience with the challenge problems led her to use the min strategy more often even on the small-addend problems.

To summarize, from the beginning of the pretest to the end of the practice phase, Whitney's main strategy was retrieval. She discovered both the shortcut-sum and the min strategy quite early in the experiment, but did not use either approach very often until she encountered the challenge problems. On the challenge problems, she consistently used the min strategy. On the mixed problem set that followed, she used the min strategy quite often, especially on large-addend problems. Thus, although she rarely used the min strategy in the sessions immediately after she discovered it, Whitney appeared to have sufficient control of the strategy to substantially increase her use of it when she encountered the challenge problems. Next, we examine a contrasting case, a child who also had used the min strategy prior to encountering the challenge problems, but who responded to them quite differently.

CHRISTIAN

At the beginning of the study, Christian, 5 years and 3 months, was a member of the kindergarten class. His pretest performance was quite average. He was correct on 80% of the problems, his median RT was 8.4 sec, and he retrieved 10% of the answers. These were, respectively, the third, seventh, and fifth highest scores of the eight children.

Christian's overall level of performance remained quite average during the course of the experiment. He was correct on 80% of items during the practice phase, slightly below the 85% for the group as a whole. This overall level masked quite dissimilar performance on small- and large-addend problems, though. Christian answered correctly on 92% of small-addend problems; this placed him above the group average of 89%, and made him the third most accurate among the eight children. In contrast, he answered only 46% of the large-addend items correctly, which was far below the group average of 76%. Only one other child did less well.

As shown in Fig. 4.4, Christian's strategy use changed substantially over time. The pattern can be seen as involving three waves of strategy use. Initially, the sum strategy was at the crest of the wave; then, finger recognition rode the crest; finally, the shortcut-sum approach became dominant.

Christian first used the min strategy in his 15th session, on the problem 4 + 1. Unfortunately, the sound on the video recorder malfunctioned on the trial, so that no protocol of the discovery could be obtained. The experimenter's notes indicated that Christian answered the problem correctly and that his use of the min strategy met the loose but not the strict criterion, but this is all that is known about the trial.

What was most interesting about Christian's performance in the experiment was not his few uses of the min strategy, but rather his experience with the shortcut-sum approach. He first used the shortcut-sum approach in his fourth session, on the problem 2 + 1. In the next 14 sessions, he used it on only 4 of 98 trials. All of these uses involved problems where 1 was an addend.

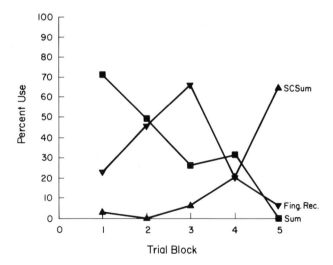

FIG. 4.4. Strategy use over trial blocks for Christian.

Then Christian encountered the challenge problems. They did not result in further uses of the min strategy; he did not use that approach either during the challenge set or for eight sessions thereafter. However, attempting to solve the challenge problems had a large and immediate effect on Christian's use of the shortcut-sum aproach. Consider his reaction to the first challenge problem:

E: *How much is 23 + 1?*

C: *23 + 1?*

E: *Yep.*

C: *Hmmm . . . 23 + 1 . . . 23 + 1?*

E: *Mhm.*

C: *23 + 1!*

E: *That's right.*

C: *Let's see . . .* (starts to count fingers on both hands) *. . . what was it?*

E: *23 + 1.*

C: (counts fingers on only one hand some more) *. . . Is it . . . 23?*

E: *Is that your answer?*

C: *Mmmm, no . . . it's 23 + 1?*

E: *23 + 1.*

C: (begins counting fingers on one hand again) *. . . 24!* (big smile).

E: *OK, how did you know that?*

C: *Because I counted my fingers.*

E: *How did you count your fingers?*

C: *23 + 1? OK, I went 1, 2, 3, 4, 5, 6, 7, 8, 9, 10, 11, 12, 13, 14, 15, 16, 17, 18, 19, 20, 21, 22* (pause), *23,* (pause and then puts up one finger on the other hand) *24.*

Not surprisingly, this trial took an extremely long time, 89 sec.

After this, Christian used the shortcut-sum approach a great deal. He employed it on 8 of 15 challenge problems. In the remaining 9 sessions, he used it on 71% of trials. In this time, he used the shortcut-sum strategy on 79% (30 of 38) of the large-addend problems and on 61% (17 of 28) of the small-addend problems. Thus, he used the approach on the small-addend problems where he previously had used other approaches, as well as on the large-addend problems that he had not previously encountered.

Although Christian used the shortcut-sum strategy extensively during this time, his use was also selective. On the small-addend problems that included 1 as an addend, he used the shortcut-sum approach on only 25% of trials (2 of 8). On the small-addend problems that did not have 1 as an addend, he used it on 75% of trials (15 of 20).

On the second to last problem of his last session of the experiment, Christian met the strict criterion for use of the min strategy. It was only the second time he had employed the min strategy, the first being 15 sessions earlier. The trial went as follows.

E: *Ok, Christian, How much is 1 + 24?*

C: *1 + 24!?*

E: *Yep.*

C: *Umm . . . . 25.*

E: *How did you know that?*

C: *I . . . counted in my head.*

E: *How did you count it in your head?*

C: *What was it again?*

E: *1 + 24.*

C: *I went . . . 1, 2, 3, 4, 5, si . . . I went, 24 + 1, I, well, ... I'll try to get you to understand, ok?*

E: *Ok.*

C: *I went 24 + 1 . . .* (whispers) *24 . .* (whispers) *25 . . that's what I did.*

E: *Ok, that's good, well why didn't you count 1, 2, 3, 4, 5, 6, 7, 8, 9, 10, all the way to 24?*

C: *Aww, that would take too long . . . silly.*

Unfortunately for our purposes, this trial came on the 208th of the 209 trials that Christian encountered in the study. This was too late to determine whether he would generalize the min strategy to additional problems or whether it, like his previous use of the min strategy, would be followed by a long period in which he never used it. The end of the preschool year prevented us from finding out.

Although this one late use of the min strategy was intriguing, the shortcut-sum strategy must play a considerably larger role in any summary of Christian's performance in the experiment. Encountering the challenge problems exercised a large effect on his strategy use, just as it did with Brittany, Lauren, and Whitney. Rather than leading him to use the min strategy, however, their initial effect, at least, was to lead him to increase his use of the shortcut-sum approach. The shortcut-sum strategy was not an ideal solution to the difficulties posed by the large addend problems. It did not enable Christian to perform very accurately; he was correct on only 66% of total trials on which he used the shortcut-sum approach and 50% of large-addend trials on which he did. Possibly, if he had not been able to use the shortcut-sum strategy, he would have learned to use the min strategy instead. It was also possible, though, that without the shortcut-sum approach, Christian might have been totally unable to cope with many of the large-addend problems. Although not as effective as the min strategy in dealing with problems such as 23 + 2, it at least allowed him to form some type of representation of large numbers that could be used to solve such problems. In a sense, it kept him in the game in situations that otherwise might have been daunting.

RUTH

Ruth was in some ways the most representative child in the sample, and in other ways the least representative. When the experiment began, she was 5 years and 7 months old, and a member of the kindergarten class. The knowledge of addition that she showed on the pretest was average for the sample. She answered 72% of items correctly, the fourth highest among the eight children. Her percent correct retrieval on the pretest, 28%, was also the fourth highest. Her median RT, 8 sec, was the fifth fastest.

In some ways, Ruth's performance remained quite representative throughout the practice phase. In particular, her 83% correct was the fourth highest among the eight children and was very close to the overall group average of 85%. However, Ruth's performance during the practice phase also diverged in important ways from that of the group as a whole. She was the only child to have serious difficulty in executing correctly the standard sum strategy. The other children ranged from 85% to 100% correct when they used it; Ruth was correct on only 67% of the trials where she did. She was the only child who was both faster and more accurate on the large-addend than on the small-addend problems. Moreover, she was the only child ever to use the strategy of counting from the first addend.

Ruth's overall distribution of strategy use was also atypical. Compared to the other children, she relied less on one or two approaches, instead spreading her strategy use relatively evenly across a number of approaches. She was the only child to use, on at least 10 trials each, six different strategies (min, sum, shortcut-sum, counting from the first addend, finger recognition, and retrieval). She used her two most common approaches, retrieval and the min strategy, on a lower percentage of trials (59%) than any of the other children used their two most common approaches. Her use of diverse strategies was evident from the first session in the practice phase, where in seven trials, she used the sum strategy, the shortcut-sum strategy, and retrieval.

Ruth was the first child to use the min strategy; she did so in her second session. Her discovery, unlike that of the other children, came at a time when she was having difficulty answering correctly by other means. After correctly answering the first problem of the session, 5 + 4, Ruth proceeded to incorrectly answer 4 + 1, 1 + 5, and 3 + 1. The four problems included uses of the sum strategy, the shortcut-sum strategy, and retrieval. On all four trials, her solution times were quite long, ranging from 16 to 30 sec.

In this context of varied strategy use, incorrect answers, and long solution times, Ruth then produced perhaps the clearest example of an insightful discovery process of any child in the experiment:

E. *How much is 4 + 3?*

R: *7*

E: *OK, that's right, very good, how did you know that?*

R: *Counted — I started with 4.*

E: *Started from 4 — Can you tell why you started from 4?*

R: *Because that's — that's — because I can um — can — I don't have to count a very long ways if I start from 4, I just have to do 3 more.*

Having produced this clear, concise rationale for using the min strategy, Ruth proceeded to construct the less efficient count-from-first-addend strategy later in the same session.

E: *How much is 2 + 3?*

R: (counts on leg and whispers) *2 . . 3 . . 4, 5, 6. Six.*

E: *OK, and how did you know that?*

R: *Counted on my tights . . . I started from 2.*

Ruth continued to use both the min and the count-from-first-addend strategies over the 12 sessions between her discovery of them and presentation of the challenge problems. During this period, she produced seven unambiguous uses of the count-from-first strategy (counting from the smaller addend on problems where the smaller addend was first, such as 2 + 4), five unambiguous uses of the min strategy (counting from the larger addend on problems where it was second, such as 2 + 5), and seven cases where both strategies would produce the same behavior (e.g., counting from the first addend on 4 + 3). There was no particular trend over these 12 sessions toward using one or the other strategy more often or of using one in one session and the other in another session. Ruth used both strategies throughout the period, and she produced unambiguous uses of both approaches in four of the sessions. She also used the sum and shortcut-sum strategies throughout the period, often using them to solve problems that she previously had solved by using the min strategy or counting from the first addend.

As with all of the children described in this chapter, Ruth's strategy use changed strikingly when she encountered the challenge problems. She used the min strategy to solve 9 of the 15 challenge problems that she was presented. She never counted on from the first addend and never used the sum strategy on them, although she did use the shortcut-sum approach three times.

When presented the mixed problems in the final nine sessions, Ruth returned to using a diverse set of strategies. The set of strategies was not quite as diverse as it had been before presentation of the challenge problems; she never again counted from the first addend when it was not also the larger addend. However, along with 10 uses of the min strategy during this period, she also used the sum and shortcut-sum strategies on seven trials apiece. As previously, there was no clear differentiation in the problems on which she used the different counting strategies. For example, on the three presentations of 3 + 9, she first used the min strategy, then the sum strategy, and then the min strategy again. Similarly, she used the min strategy to solve 5 + 2 and 7 + 2, but used the shortcut-sum strategy on both presentations of 6 + 2.

On the surface, Ruth's overall pattern of performance may seem paradoxical. She combined average pretest performance with being the first child to discover the min strategy; insightful discovery of the min strategy with use of the less efficient count-from-first-addend strategy later in the same session; difficulty in executing the sum strategy with continued use of the sum strategy when the min approach was also available to her. These facts defy an easy summary. The combination may not be as surprising as it initially appears, however. Ruth's willingness to use diverse strategies throughout the experiment may have stemmed from the same dispositions that led to her being the first child to discover the min strategy and the only child to use the count-from-first-addend approach. It may not always be the child with the most advanced knowledge who first discovers a new strategy. Willingness to consider diverse strategies and to continue using them even when they are not working perfectly may also help determine which children are the innovators.

CONCLUDING COMMENTS

Case studies are associated more closely with clinical than with cognitive psychology. Clinical patients vary along so many dimensions that detailed descriptions of individual cases have long been recognized as essential. We suspect that understanding of cognition might also benefit from detailed analyses of individual cases and comparison of them to similarly detailed analyses of other individuals' reactions to the same experiences.

Case studies have several clear advantages for studying cognition. One is that they can communicate a sense of the quality of the cognitive activity that is being examined. Cognition is more than reaction times, accuracy rates, and frequency of use of strategies. Although many researchers informally ask their subjects what they were thinking during the experiment, the replies rarely find their way into any formal report of the results. Reductions of the verbal reports to numbers can reveal common trends, but sacrifices qualitative information that can play a critical role in constraining and guiding theory construction. Especially for describing unusual or novel cognitive activities, such as generating a new strategy and using it for the first time, allowing subjects to describe the experience in their own words may be invaluable to our understanding of their thinking. For example, the protocols of children discovering new strategies or applying them to new classes of problems convey a sense of the strained and halting nature of the breakthroughs. The particular manifestations varied: Whitney and Brittany explicitly denied that they had counted before they correctly described the counting they had done; Christian had to have the problem repeated four times before he used the shortcut-sum strategy for the first time; Christian also felt compelled to say "I'll try to get you to understand, ok" when trying to explain his first use of the min strategy to the strict criterion; Lauren's description included numerous "ums" and repetitions of words. Reporting the speed and accuracy characteristics of these trials only scratches the surface of the cognitive activity that was occurring. The children's own words allow us a deeper understanding.

The present case studies also illustrated both the common trends and the exceptions to these trends that were evident in this study. For most children, initial discovery of the min strategy was followed by little use of the strategy prior to the challenge problems. Ruth, however, used both the min strategy and the related count-from-first-addend strategy often during this period. Encountering the challenge problems influenced the performance of all five of the children whose cases were described in this chapter, and was followed by greater use of the min strategy in four of the five cases. But Christian increased his use of the shortcut-sum approach, rather than that of the min strategy, and two children whose cases were not described showed no apparent effects of being presented the challenge problems. On the mixed problem set that followed the challenge problems, most children used the min strategy primarily on the large-addend problems and retrieved answers to most of the small-addend problems. Brittany, however, used the min strategy on the majority of both small- and large-addend problems in this period.

The child-to-child variability could also be seen in relations among different measures of knowledge. A high percentage of retrieval was in general a sign of advanced knowledge of addition, and typically was accompanied by a high degree of accuracy. From the beginning to the end of the experiment, however, Whitney had the highest frequency of retrieval of all of the children, despite consistently answering less accurately than most. Similarly, with increasing practice, and presumably increasing knowledge, most children move toward more frequent use of retrieval and toward less frequent use of the sum strategy. Lauren reversed these tendencies, however, until she encountered the challenge problems.

The variability was also evident in the behavior that surrounded the transition to use of the min strategy. Most children produced long solution times on the trial on which they first used the min strategy and on the immediately preceding trials. Brittany did not. Similarly, most children discovered the min strategy in the same session in which they discovered the shortcut-sum approach or soon thereafter. Christian, though, did not use the min strategy for 11 sessions after he began to use the shortcut-sum approach, and did not use it a second time until he had used the shortcut-sum approach on 70 trials. We strongly suspect that this pattern will prove to be quite general. The more detailed information that we obtain about individual subjects' strategy construction processes, the more inescapable will be the variability in the way they construct the new strategies. We also suspect that this statement will hold true for change processes in general and for adults as well as children. The more information we have available about individual subjects' change processes, regardless of their age, the more evident will be individual variation in the process.

5

Summary, Conclusions, and Ideas

The present research yielded a detailed portrayal of how children construct one strategy. Although it is always dangerous to extrapolate from a single instance, many features of construction of this strategy seemed likely to be widely shared. Therefore, in this final chapter, we use observations from the study not only to draw conclusions about how children generate the min strategy but also to suggest hypotheses about strategy construction in general.

The chapter is divided into four sections. First we consider factors leading up to discovery of a new strategy. Then we examine the process of discovery itself. Following this, the focus turns to how newly discovered strategies are generalized beyond the initial context in which they were first applied. Finally, we address what is perhaps the central question raised by this study: What strategy construction mechanisms lead children to generate appropriate new strategies, yet not to generate inappropriate ones?

PRECURSORS OF DISCOVERY

Strategy Use

Before the 4- and 5-year-olds in this study discovered the min strategy, they already knew several ways to add numbers. These prior strategies did not only provide means for solving problems. They also provided a basis for constructing new strategies and shaped the kinds of problems on which children used the min strategy once they discovered it. Thus, as is generally the case, the acquisition process can best be understood in the context of prior knowledge.

It seems useful to think of the strategies that people know for solving a class of problems as forming a kind of ecology. The strategies that already populate the cognitive environment compete in ways that shape the types of problems on which new strategies will be used. Two key influences are the accuracy and efficiency with which each strategy can be executed on a given problem or class of problems. For example, a new strategy may generate answers accurately and efficiently on a problem, but if an already-known strategy can solve that problem equally accurately and even more efficiently, the new strategy will rarely be used on the problem. Similarly, a strategy may be used often on a class of problems not because it works particularly well on them but because no other strategy works well at all.

What was the ecology of preschoolers' addition strategies like before they discovered the min strategy? For most children, the competitors included the sum strategy, the shortcut-sum strategy, finger recognition, retrieval, and guessing. The environments in which these strategies competed were small-number addition problems, problems with addends of 5 or less. Strategies competed for use even within a single problem, and different strategies were selected on different occasions. For example, Ruth was presented the problem 5 + 3 nine times in the course of the experiment. Starting from the first presentation, she used the following strategies to solve it: retrieval, the min strategy, the min strategy again, retrieval, the shortcut-sum strategy, the sum strategy, finger recognition, the sum strategy, and the shortcut-sum strategy. Two aspects of this sequence are notable: that she used five different strategies on the nine presentations of the problem, and that the sequence was in no way a unidirectional progression from use of less-advanced strategies to use of more advanced ones. Other children showed similar patterns; for example, Brittany used the same five strategies in her 12 presentations of 5 + 1.

This view of cognitive development as competition among diverse strategies differs from the traditional view that children progress from using Strategy A to using Strategy B to using Strategy C (or from Stage I to II to III, or from Rule 1 to 2 to 3). Clearly, in young children's arithmetic, more- and less-advanced strategies coexist and continue to compete over an extended period of time. Nor is the phenomenon of multiple strategy use unique to the present study, to arithmetic, or to 4- and 5-year-olds. For example, Payne (1976) documented that many adults use multiple decision-making strategies, Shultz et al. (1986) documented that 7- and 8-year-olds use multiple causal inference strategies, and Maratsos (1983) documented that 1- and 2-year-olds use a variety of strategies for generating plural and past tense language forms.

Although all of the children in the present study used multiple strategies, it was also true that over the course of the experiment, children increasingly used the more advanced strategies. That is, with practice in solving arithmetic problems, children slowly moved from more use of the less-advanced strategies, such as guessing and the sum strategy, to more use of the more-advanced strategies, such as the min strategy and retrieval. As noted in chapter 4, the movement can be likened to a wave, in which the direction of change was always from less- to more-advanced strategies, but the particular strategies at the crest of the wave changed over time. The wavelike character of the changes could be seen most clearly within individual children's performance. For example, at the outset of the experiment, Christian most often used the sum strategy; later, he most often used finger recognition; still later, he most often used the shortcut-sum approach. At all times, he used several different strategies, but the modal strategy changed over time.

This picture of strategy use at any one time and of changes in strategy use over time is consistent with portrayals that have emerged from studies of long-term learning in a number of other domains. These include such varied areas as scientific reasoning (Kuhn, Amsel, & O'Laughlin, 1988; Kuhn & Phelps, 1982), serial recall of long lists of numbers (Chase & Ericsson, 1981; Ericsson et al., 1980), mental multiplication (Staszewski, 1987), and writing of LOGO programs (Lawler, 1985). For example, Kuhn's descriptions of 10- and 11-year-olds' strategies for solving scientific reasoning problems could be applied almost verbatim to our observations of 4- and 5-year-olds' strategies for solving simple addition problems:

> Every subject showed a mixed inference strategy pattern in at least one session, and most often over repeated sessions. . . . Competence in executing advanced strategies was not a sufficient condition for problem mastery, and co-occurrence of valid and invalid strategies within a single session proved to be the rule rather than the exception. (Kuhn & Phelps, 1982, p. 24)

> More- and less-advanced strategies clearly coexisted in Randy's cognitive repertory, and it was impossible to predict with certainty which

would surface at any particular point. Yet, gradually the more advanced strategies became prevalent. (Kuhn et al., 1988, p. 191)

These observations, like our own, suggest that new strategies often do not enter a vacuum; rather, they become members of groups of competing entities within the larger ecology of strategies.

Immediate Precursors of Discovery

Microgenetic Methods and the Study of Transitions. Because the microgenetic method used in the present study allowed identification of each child's first use of the min strategy, it also allowed examination of what led up to the discoveries. Two consistent patterns characterized performance just before the discoveries: long solution times and appearance of the shortcut-sum strategy.

On the trial immediately before discovery of the min strategy, average solution times were twice as long as the average for the experiment as a whole. The long solution times might be interpreted as indicating that the problems were very difficult. This was not the case, however; they were quite representative of the total set of problems that children encountered in the study. Further, the same child often had solved the same problem much more rapidly and without any obvious difficulty earlier in the experiment.

What, then, led to the long solution times? One possibility is that they resulted from conflict or interference among competing strategies. The many partial executions of strategies, pauses, and strange statements that occurred on the trials just before the discoveries suggested that such difficulty was occurring. For example, on a problem such as 5 + 4, a child might audibly count "1, 2, 3," pause for 10 seconds, ask for the problem to be repeated, and then solve the problem by counting from 1 to 9. Children did not say much about the contents of their thinking during the long period before their answers, and a high percentage of what they did say was difficult to interpret. However, the unusually long times and the behaviors that could be seen and heard on these trials suggested that some type of cognitive conflict or interference was occurring.

A second consistent pattern in the period immediately preceding the initial use of the min strategy involved transitional strategies. Most children first used the shortcut-sum strategy in the session or two just before they first used the min strategy. The nature of the shortcut-sum strategy made it a very plausible transitional approach between the sum and the min strategies, in the sense that it incorporated features of both old and new procedures. It was like the sum strategy in that it involved starting at one and counting all of the numbers between one and the sum of the addends. It was like the min strategy in that the representation of the second addend and its addition to the running total took place simultaneously (on 5 + 2, the shortcut-sum strategy would involve counting "1, 2, 3, 4, 5, *6, 7*" rather than "1, 2, 3, 4, 5," "1, 2," "1, 2, 3, 4, 5, 6, 7." Thus, the shortcut-sum strategy provided a potential bridge between the sum and the min approaches.

In addition to its surface plausibility as a transitional strategy, two types of evidence pointed to the shortcut-sum strategy often playing such a mediating role: almost all of the children used the shortcut-sum approach, and most of them first used it shortly before discovering the min strategy. It would be interesting to test experimentally the hypothesized role of the shortcut-sum approach by teaching it to a randomly chosen group of children who did not yet know the min strategy and determining if they discovered the min strategy more quickly than peers who had not been not taught the hypothesized transitional approach.

These findings and hypotheses about immediate precursors of the discovery were made possible by the microgenetic method that we used. Without a method that allowed children's performance to be intensely scrutinized on a trial-by-trial basis over an extended period of time, many of the findings could not have emerged. This conclusion can be illustrated by contrasting the results that emerged with our approach to the ones that emerged in previous studies that relied entirely on chronometric methods to study the same transition.

Groen and Resnick (1977) hypothesized that the count-from-first-addend strategy would be involved in the transition from the sum to the min approach. Their chronometric analyses of individual subjects' data from successive blocks of 125 trials showed that at no point was the size of the second addend, the predictor associated with this hypothesized transitional strategy, the best predictor of solution times. As they pointed out, however, this did not necessarily mean that counting from the first addend was not critical to the transition. If children counted from the first addend only for a short time or only on some problems, the predictor associated with the strategy would not have shown up in the chronometric analysis. This possibility seemed sufficiently plausible that Resnick and Neches (1984) later formulated a computer simulation model in which counting from the first addend was the key transitional strategy.

One advantage of microgenetic methods is that they can rule out hypotheses about transition strategies. Had Groen and Resnick used a microgenetic rather than a chronometric approach, and rarely or never observed any child using the hypothesized transition strategy before using the min strategy, they and future theorists would have been unlikely to make this strategy critical within a theory of how the transition occurs.

The microgenetic method was also critical to our hypothesis concerning the role of the shortcut-sum strategy. Within a chronometric analysis, or any other analysis using structural features of the problem to predict performance, the sum and shortcut-sum strategies would look identical. The best predictor of solution times and percentage of errors on each problem for both strategies would be the size of the sum. Only an approach that examined the counting that was actually done on each trial could reveal the difference between them. Further, only a longitudinal approach could suggest a linkage between the shortcut-sum and min strategies, by revealing the rapidity with which discovery of the min strategy usually followed discovery of the shortcut-sum approach.

In general, the microgenetic method seems sensitive to a broader array of changes than alternative, more frequently used methodologies. Greater use of the method could trigger improvement in the quality of developmental theorizing, both by revealing crucial mediators of change and by seriously constraining the forms that plausible theories about transitions can take. Thus, where questions about transition processes are central, the microgenetic approach seems to be the method of choice.

The Role of Impasses and Wrong Answers. Investigators have noted a variety of external events that lead people to construct new strategies. Receiving explicit instruction in how to execute new approaches, observing other people using them, and encountering analogous strategies in other contexts are three of the most commonly discussed external influences (Anderson, 1983; Holland et al., 1986; MacWhinney, 1978). Probably the prototypic instance, however, involves negative feedback. A subject advances incorrect answers, learns that the answers are wrong, and tries a new approach. The negative feedback is seen as creating an impasse that leads learners to generate alternative strategies and to think more deeply about why the previous strategy failed.

Perhaps the most surprising finding of the present study was that discovery of the min strategy was not especially likely to be preceded by wrong answers, inability to generate any answer, or negative feedback. Both in terms of performance on the trial immediately preceding the first use of the strategy and in terms of performance on all previous trials in the session in which the new strategy was discovered, errors were no more likely than would be expected from the overall percent incorrect for all problems. Five of the seven children who discovered the min strategy did so without having made any errors in that session.

At first impression, this finding seems at odds with results from hypothesis-testing tasks (e.g., Gholson, Levine, & Phillips, 1972; Levine, 1966) that new strategies are generated almost exclusively when existing approaches fail to produce correct predictions. The finding also seems to contradict a large body of data on physical and social science reasoning tasks, indicating that children are more likely to construct new strategies when they encounter problems that disconfirm existing approaches (e.g., Collins & Stevens, 1982; Inhelder et al., 1974; Richards, 1982; Siegler, 1976). Finally, the finding seems totally at odds with artificial-intelligence and theoretical-linguistics models of strategy construction (e.g., Newell's, in press, SOAR model; VanLehn's, 1988, RT2 model; and Berwick's, 1985, syntax acquisition model). VanLehn (1988) stated clearly these models' assumption about learning of new procedures. "Learning occurs only when an impasse occurs. If there is no impasse, there is no learning" (pp. 31–32).

What might account for the differences between the past findings and the present ones? One possibility is that different types of strategies are constructed in response to different circumstances. Two types of strategy changes can be distinguished: changes in which the main difference between the strategies is in the answers themselves, and changes in which the main differences are not in the answers that are generated but rather in the efficiency with which answers are generated and/or the aesthetic appeal of the procedures. The first type of strategy change may occur primarily as a result of encountering impasses, but the second may typically occur for other reasons.

Changes in strategies for solving liquid quantity conservation problems illustrate the first type of development. Children switch from choosing the glass with the taller liquid column, a strategy that produces consistently wrong answers on the classic Piagetian problems, to relying on the reasoning that pouring does not alter quantity, an approach that produces correct answers. The studies that have indicated that negative feedback and impasses lead to generation of new strategies generally involve this type of transition. For example, feedback that answers were incorrect has led to children rejecting conservation, class inclusion, transitive inference, balance scale, and duration rules that do not consistently produce correct answers in favor of ones that always do (Brainerd, 1974; Gelman, 1969; Siegler, 1976, 1983).

In contrast, in the present situation, existing strategies such as the sum and shortcut-sum approaches are comparable to the min strategy in ability to generate correct answers. All three strategies in principle can always produce correct performance and in fact generally did so in this study (see Table 3.3). The advantage of the min strategy over the other two approaches is primarily in the efficiency with which the correct answer can be generated, and perhaps in its aesthetic appeal (as reflected in Brittany's comment "smart answer" following her first use of the min strategy), rather than in probability of generating correct answers.[1]

Although most research on cognitive development has focused on strategy changes that produce greater accuracy, both types of changes are actually quite common. Even within a single task, some transitions can involve changes in accuracy and others changes in efficiency. For example, in number conservation, an early transition involves a change from responding on the basis of the relative length of the rows of objects to responding on the basis of counting the objects in each row or matching them in 1:1 correspondence (Siegler, 1981). This transition enhances ability to generate correct answers. A later transition on the same task involves a change from relying on counting or 1:1 correspondence to deducing answers from the type of transformation that was performed. This transition change the efficiency with which correct answers can be generated, and seems more elegant, but has little if any effect on the likelihood of generating the correct response (both approaches consistently produce correct responses).

Markman (1978) described a similar pair of transitions in class inclusion. The earlier transition involves changing from comparing the number of objects in two subordinate classes (dogs and cats) to comparing the number of objects in a subordinate class to that in its superordinate class (dogs and animals). This transition results in a

---

[1]On certain problems, such as 22 + 2, the min strategy is more accurate as well as more efficient. Note, however, that only one child discovered the min strategy on such a problem. Most discovered it on problems such as 4 + 3, where new and old strategies yielded equally accurate performance.

change from consistently incorrect to consistently correct responding. A later change involves a switch from basing answers on the outcomes of counting to basing them on the reasoning that the superordinate set necessarily includes more objects. As in number conservation, this strategy change improves the efficiency with which correct answers can be generated, and seems more elegant, but has no effect on accuracy.

In summary, the common view that impasses are essential for learning needs to be modified. Failure of existing strategies to produce correct answers may usually accompany generation of strategies whose main contribution is greater accuracy. However, the present experiment demonstrates that impasses are not essential for discovery of strategies whose main contributions are greater efficiency and/or elegance. Neither inability to generate any answer nor production of incorrect answers nor reception of negative feedback were typical, much less necessary, precursors of children's discovery of the min strategy.

THE DISCOVERY ITSELF

Regularity and Variability in Strategy Discovery

Detailed scrutiny of the trial on which each child first used the min strategy revealed both regularities and variability. The regularities can be quickly summarized. Solution times on discovery trials tended to be much longer than average. They also were considerably longer than would have been expected from the types of problems on which the discoveries occurred. False starts, long pauses, and slow counting all accompanied many children's discoveries.

The variability in children's discovery processes was more striking than the commonalities. All types of problems, from very easy to very hard, sometimes triggered discovery of the min strategy. Some children discovered the new strategy in the first week of the study, whereas others did not discover it anytime during the 11 weeks of practice. The quality of the discoveries also varied greatly. Some children showed little or no awareness that they had done anything new; others clearly realized that they had used a new strategy and could aptly explain why the new strategy was a good one (e.g., "because then you don't have to count all those numbers").

The large amount of variability in children's discovery processes may seem surprising. However, similar variability is evident in other accounts of discovery, notably in accounts of the discovery processes of great scientists (e.g., Nickles, 1978). This variability is one factor that has given rise to the view that there is no normative logic to scientific discovery. For example, Popper (1959) argued that "The initial stage, the act of conceiving or inventing a theory, seems to me neither to call for logical analysis nor to be susceptible of it. . . . There is no such thing as a logical method for having new ideas or a logical reconstruction of this process (pp. 31–32).[2] Some scientific discoveries have involved inductive generalizations from data (e.g., Boyle's gas laws); others have been deductions from theoretical assumptions (e. g., Michaelson and Morley's test of general relativity theory); some have involved sudden insights (e.g., Kekule's discovery of the benzene ring); others have had a more gradual cumulative flavor (e. g., Darwin's evolutionary theory); and so on. Both noble scientific discoveries and mundane everyday discoveries seem to be based on opportunistic, catch-as-catch-can cognitive processes that take a variety of forms and occur in a variety of situations. Both provide evidence for Klahr's (1984) hypothesis that comparable end points of understanding often mask considerable diversity in the acquisition process.

Why does this variability in strategy discovery occur? Klahr (1984) attributed it to variation in people's experiences. Although this is undoubtedly an important source of variability in everyday environments, it does not explain why the discoveries of children given almost identical experiences in a laboratory study, such as the present one, would vary so much. A possible rejoinder would be that variability in pre-experimental experience may have produced the variable strategy constructions. This hypothesis is difficult to evaluate without specification of the critical pre-experimental experiences, however. The weak relations between our measures of children's pre-experimental numerical knowledge and their subsequent strategy constructions also were not encouraging signs for this hypothesis.

It may be useful to think about the problem by adopting the opposite perspective. From this vantage point, variability, rather than regularity, is seen as the norm. This alternative view leads us to change the question from "Given that there is so much regularity in the end

---

[2]However, see Hanson (1961) and Langley, Simon, Bradshaw, and Zytkow (1987) for contrary views.

products of cognitive growth, why is there so much variability early in the acquisition process?" to "Given that there is so much variability in the acquisition process, why is there so much regularity in the end products of cognitive growth?"

This question has an answer that is both simple and general. The answer emphasizes the formative influence of the environment after a discovery has been made. Specifically, the effectiveness of strategies in solving problems almost certainly contributes to convergence from variable initial points to regular end points. To illustrate, one child who discovered the min strategy might initially use it on a wide variety of problems; another might use it on few problems of any kind. Through experience using the min strategy and other approaches, however, both children would learn that the min strategy was particularly useful on problems where the smaller addend was small and the difference between the addends was large. Both also would learn that the min strategy takes longer to execute than retrieval, and that on most problems, it takes less time than counting from one. Thus, the way in which strategies interact with the problems on which they are used seems likely to channel initial variability into later regularity.

Hemming and Hawing at the Point of Discovery

Although the children in our study usually could accurately describe the strategy they used on each trial, they often became strikingly less articulate on the trial on which they discovered the new strategy. As on the trial immediately before the discovery, pauses, incomplete sentences, and multiple starts and stops characterized these discovery trials. Some self-reports on the discovery trials directly contradicted the evidence of the children's overt behavior, as when they could be heard counting but said "Never counted." Other strategy descriptions were partially consistent with overt behavior on the trial and partially inconsistent, as when a child could be heard counting "4, 5, 6, 7" but said that she counted "3, add one is 4, add one is 5, add one is 6, add one is 7, add one is 8." Yet other self-reports such as "I just blobbed around" conveyed no information whatsoever. Thus, the clarity of children's self-reports was lowest precisely where we wished it to be highest, on their first use of the new strategy.

Such inarticulateness may not just be an unfortunate feature of children's discovery of the min strategy. Indeed, it may accompany many strategy discoveries. Generating a new strategy almost certainly requires more mental resources than using a well-established one. This would leave fewer resources available for monitoring exactly what had been done and generating the words to describe the activities. The new strategy may also be executed amid partial executions of the old one; Whitney's and Brittany's initial denials that they counted when they first used the min strategy, in the face of audible evidence of their counting, may have been due to their having been almost able to retrieve the answer to the problem, and to their thinking that they had succeeded in doing so. A further complexity of describing newly discovered strategies is that since the strategy is new, there will be no previously developed verbal label for describing it. Both understanding the new procedure well enough to identify its important components and finding a label or concise description for characterizing it may be difficult. Thus, demands on mental resources, incomplete segregation of new strategies from previous ones, lack of conceptual understanding of the new acquisition, and absence of labels for describing it may all conspire to make it difficult for people to describe their new discoveries.

Why Don't Children Discover Bad Strategies?

As striking as the strategies that children discovered were those that they did not discover. Not one child adopted a strategy that could be classified as indicating a lack of understanding of the goals of addition. Several imaginable illegitimate strategies were procedurally similar to legitimate strategies and therefore might have been expected to be tried. For example, children might have been expected to try counting the first addend twice, counting the second addend twice, starting from the cardinal value of the smaller addend and counting on by the value of the smaller addend, or counting on from the first addend by the amount indicated by the first addend. Yet not one child used these or other illegitimate strategies, even on a single trial. What constrained them from even trying such strategies in this situation?

The claim is not that children never generated flawed addition procedures. They occasionally did. However, the incorrectness of these procedures arose from difficulties in their efforts to meet appropriate goals, rather than from adoption of inappropriate goals. This can be illustrated with reference to a strategy that arose when children encountered problems on which one of the addends was larger than 5, such as 7 + 2. To solve this problem, most children represented the seven by putting up five fingers on one hand and two on the other. At this point, however, some children became confused about how to represent the second addend. A procedure that two children adopted was to put down the fingers on the hand that earlier had all five fingers up and then to represent the second addend by putting up two fingers on that hand. Following this, both children counted the two fingers that were up on each hand and answered "4." The procedure failed to maintain the original representation of each addend until the problem was solved, and the answer violated the rule that adding two positive numbers must result in a sum greater than either addend. However, these violations seemed to grow out of efforts to conform to the core goals of addition: representing each addend in a quantifiable form and then quantifying the combined representation. Moreover, the children who used this approach seemed unhappy at having spoiled their representation of the one addend in order to represent the other.

The avoidance of strategies that violate basic goals or principles has been documented in domains other than arithmetic. One well-known example involves counting of objects. Gelman and Gallistel (1978) presented children an order-irrelevance task, in which the children needed to devise nonstandard counting techniques that would meet criteria external to those of standard counting. For example, the children might need to count in such a way that the second object from the left would be the fifth in the counting sequence. Children often did not succeed in meeting all of the demands. However, the methods they devised showed clear attempts to conform to the basic goals of counting as well as to the stipulations of the task. That is, they attempted to assign one and only one number to each object and to state the numbers in the correct order.

The task for a strategy generation mechanism is to show not only how the strategies that children discover could be discovered but also to explain why on some tasks, such as counting and simple addition, many possible illegitimate strategies are not discovered. The final section of this chapter (the section titled "Strategy Construction Mechanisms") describes a mechanism that could contribute to both discovery of useful strategies and avoidance of illegitimate ones.

GENERALIZATION OF NEWLY DISCOVERED STRATEGIES

The first use of the min strategy proved to be only the beginning of the strategy construction process. Even children who eventually became frequent users of the strategy tended to use it rarely in the period immediately after the discovery. For example, the child who eventually used the min strategy on the highest percentage of trials of any of the participants used it on only 7 of the first 84 trials following her discovery of it. Similarly, the child who eventually used the min strategy on the second highest percentage of trials used it on only 2 of 49 trials following her initial use.

The slow uptake of the new strategy that was evident in most children's performance ran counter to the everyday "Eureka" stereotype of strategy discovery. Within this stereotype, discovery entails immediate application of the new approach. Innovations may sometimes prompt such immediate use, but they clearly do not always do so. Because the present method allowed identification of when the new strategy was first used, it also allowed us to document just how halting the strategy's generalization was.

Findings from this study also raised a number of intriguing questions regarding strategy generalization. What does it mean to say that a child has discovered a strategy? How do impasses influence the generalization process? What role does conscious insight play? These questions are the focus of the following discussion.

What Constitutes a Discovery?

Who discovered America: Leif Ericson or Christopher Columbus? If discovery is defined in terms of temporal priority, Ericson clearly should be credited. Yet it is Columbus whose contribution we celebrate. This is due in part to tradition, but also in part to the fact that Columbus' voyages stimulated a considerable amount of further exploration and settlement, whereas Ericson's did not.

Just as it is tempting to weigh identifiable consequences in deciding who discovered a geographic entity, it also is tempting to consider such consequences in deciding when a strategy has been discovered. From this perspective, it might be argued that children did not really discover the min strategy until they started using it reasonably often. The early uses might be classified as a kind of premature discovery (Hallam, 1975), and not be viewed as reflecting the same phenomenon as the later ones.

Although such a classification is tempting, it also is probably unwise. To equate discovery of a strategy with anything other than the first use of the strategy would make arbitrary any attempt to specify when the discovery occurred. How much use is enough use to conclude that a strategy has been discovered? Describing early, isolated applications of a strategy as "premature" provides a label but little else.

A better approach might be to recognize that discovery of a strategy often is only the first step toward understanding it. As with the new honors to which Banquo referred in the opening quotation of the book, understanding often comes only with use. Only as people employ new concepts and strategies, and observe their consequences in the world, do they achieve a deep understanding of the strategies' advantages, disadvantages, and conditions of applicability.

Use may be especially critical to children's understanding. Children may generally be less able than adults to anticipate the properties of a novel approach. This may doom them to "re-discover" the same idea a number of times before they understand it sufficiently to use it appropriately.

Even granting the possibility that children may be especially susceptible to the problem, it is clear that adults also are far from immune. Like children, we often discover new approaches, only to lose and subsequently rediscover them. How many times have we thought that we had generated a new insight into a problem, only to learn subsequently that it was essentially identical to ideas that we had read or generated ourselves years earlier? If someone were recording our lives with a videorecorder, our activities, like those of children in the present experiment, might prove to involve numerous false springs, situations in which an initial insight was followed by long hiatuses and sporadic applications. Even the greatest of innovators are vulnerable to this phenomenon. Wegener (1929/1966), the father of tectonic plate theory, attributed the formulation of his theory to his being struck in 1910 and 1911 "by the congruence of the coastlines of either side of the Atlantic" (1929/1966, p. 1). Yet Giere (1988) noted that a friend from Wegener's school days recalled Wegener having being struck by this congruence as early as 1903, when they were both students. As Giere wrote, "If that is so, the idea lay fallow in Wegener's brain for a long time before 1911" (p. 230). With great scientists as with children, ideas may be fully understood only with use.

But what leads to early, isolated uses of a strategy or idea becoming more frequent? Part of the answer probably is the cumulative effects of simply using the new approach and obtaining data about its effectiveness. Part also may be experiences using it that trigger deeper, more elaborative thinking about it (Bransford & Stein, 1984). One type of experience that may often produce such elaboration is discussed in the next section.

The Role of Impasses

Earlier, we argued that impasses were not necessary for discovering new strategies, in particular, strategies whose main contributions were greater efficiency and/or elegance. The situation may be very different, however, regarding generalization of previously discovered strategies.

In the present study, the challenge problems were designed to create an impasse and to motivate children to think about how they could get around it. The basic logic was that children could easily solve problems such as 22 + 3 if they used the min strategy but would have great difficulty solving them by any of the other strategies they knew. Thus, this type of problem represented both a carrot and a stick.

Many children's performance changed dramatically when they encountered the challenge problems. Children began to use the min strategy much more often than they had previously. This was not due to the challenge problems being especially effective in promoting discoveries. No child first used the min strategy during the challenge set. Rather, the effectiveness of these problems lay in their leading children who had already discovered the min strategy to use it more often. Of the five children who had used the min strategy previously, four greatly increased their use of it when they encountered the challenge set. All four continued to use it more often than before on the mixed problems that followed the challenge set. Three of the four children actually used the min strategy on a higher percentage of the mixed problems than on the problems in the challenge set.

These findings suggest that impasses play an important role in learning, but not necessarily the role that usually has been attributed to them. Impasses seem especially effective in stimulating the use of strategies that have been used occasionally in previous situations. People may discover many strategies, but not use most of them very often. Impasses may make accessible these previously uncommon approaches. The increased accessibility may come through impasses motivating more elaborated encoding and memory representations of the strategies themselves, the sources of difficulty posed by problems, and the linkages between goals and procedures that can satisfy them. When similar problems are encountered in the future, the stronger links between goals and strategies make the strategies easier to access.

This greater accessibility would lead to greater subsequent use of the previously uncommon strategies.

One of us experienced such a process recently while playing tennis. After repeatedly hitting forehands too high and too far, a long-ago strategy for dealing with this problem came to mind: waiting for the ball a little longer so that it would be parallel to the body at the point of impact. The longer wait resulted in better shots, which led to some consideration of why the strategy had this effect. This was not quite the end of the story, however. When the same problem arose in a game a few days later, it still took about 20 minutes before the problem was correctly diagnosed. This diagnosis led to the remedial strategy being applied earlier in the set than it had been a few days before, but the application was still far from immediate. Although the strategy had been recently re-discovered, further rediscoveries seemed necessary before it would be quickly adopted.

STRATEGY CONSTRUCTION MECHANISMS

In the first section of this book, we likened children's minds to a workshop. This metaphor captured a number of characteristics that seem critical to the discovery process: the construction of new knowledge from existing tools and materials; the large amount of self-motivated activity that leads to discoveries even when the situation does not demand them; the frequent need to meet challenges posed by novel problems; and so on. In this concluding section, we speculate about mechanisms by which a system with these properties might construct new strategies.

Our account begins with the hypothesis that generation of new strategies is governed by a *goal sketch*. After considering the content that might be included within a goal sketch for addition, we consider the materials that are available for meeting the objectives specified within the sketch and the mechanisms that might be used to put them together. Finally, based on our findings and analyses, we discuss properties that a general theory of strategy construction should possess.

The Goal Sketch

General Characteristics. At least in the present situation, children were able to generate appropriate new strategies without attempting unreasonable alternatives. They clearly were not proceeding by trial and error or haphazardly combining subroutines from existing procedures. What type of mechanism could serve this function of keeping new candidate strategies "on track?"

We believe that a *goal sketch* is one such mechanism. A goal sketch specifies the hierarchy of objectives that a satisfactory strategy must meet. The hierarchical structure directs searches of existing knowledge for procedures that can meet the goals. When such procedures have been identified, they are assembled into a new strategy.

Goal sketches could contribute both to discovery of useful new strategies and to avoidance of flawed approaches. As long as the objectives within a goal sketch are appropriate, the sketch should help both to direct search toward procedures that meet appropriate goals and to direct search away from procedures that do not meet essential objectives. In addition to constraining the generation of new strategies, they also provide a test against which the likely usefulness of potential strategies can be measured. A strategy that does not meet the basic goals need not be given further consideration.

The inherent structure of the task domain is not the only source of goal-related stipulations. The social or physical environment can also constrain new procedures. For example, in Gelman and Gallistel's (1978) order-invariance experiment that was described previously, children needed to obey the usual rules of counting and also to assign a given object a number that it would not receive as a part of standard left-to-right or right-to-left counting. Thus, the second object from the left in a row of four objects might need to be assigned the number "2" within the count. Making goal sketches permeable to such requirements would allow new strategies to be tailored to the demands of particular situations, while also conforming to the basic rules for acceptable strategies in the domain.

The goal sketch is a close cousin of the goal hierarchy control structure proposed by Newell and his colleagues (Newell, in press; Rosenbloom & Newell, 1986). It differs primarily in that the hierarchical levels of the goal sketch exist prior to, and apart from, the procedures used to meet the goals. In this way, it is more like the retrieval structures hypothesized by Staszewski (1987, 1988). Specifically, we believe that people can sometimes generate sketches of the goals that successful strategies in a domain must meet even when they do not know procedures for meeting the goals. They do this on the basis of general knowledge of the domain and through abstraction of the goals that are met by other successful strategies in it. This hypothesized process contrasts with Newell's depiction of the goal hierarchies as arising from the ways in which impasses were met in the particular processing episode in which the goal hierarchy was formed and as being accompanied at all times by the procedures that were used to meet the goals. The two constructs have complementary strengths and weaknesses. Newell's goal hierarchies have a broader range of applicability, since they do not depend on prior understanding of what is important in the domain. Where the present type of goal sketches can be formed, however, they provide a way of avoiding inappropriate strategies that will arise at times within the goal hierarchy approach (unless problem spaces are engineered so inappropriate strategies cannot be formed).

An Example. The potential usefulness of the goal sketch idea can be illustrated in the context of discovery of the min strategy. Figure 5.1 is a sketch of the goals that an addition strategy needs to meet. Any strategy that can meet all goals at or above a level of the hierarchy is legitimate. Thus, retrieval is a legitimate strategy because it can meet the highest goal of generating a number that quantitatively represents the combined sets. The sum strategy is perhaps the prototypic strategy within this representation, because it meets each of the goals at all three levels, and its subprocedures map onto the goals in a very transparent manner.

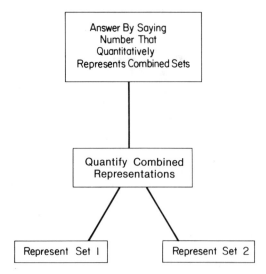

FIG. 5.1. Primal sketch for addition.

How would people acquire such goal sketches? The process seems likely to begin with learning of a procedure for achieving a general goal (e.g., adding numbers). Recognizing the subgoals that are met by each part of the procedure would produce a more detailed representation of the strategy. Acquiring alternative strategies for operating in the domain would allow the learner to further refine the goal sketch through abstracting the common goals met by all successful strategies.

What if a goal sketch were incorrect? In this case, use of the strategies that the goal sketch helped to generate seems likely to exercise a corrective influence. For example, a goal sketch that omitted necessary properties of successful strategies in a domain would allow incorrect approaches to be generated. The incorrect performance that would follow from such procedures would provide feedback relevant to the goal sketch, in that correct goal sketches should not give rise to flawed strategies. Such feedback would be relatively indirect, because unsuccessful performance might have other causes. Poor execution of a sound strategy or faulty application of a sound goal sketch would also result in poor performance. Thus, credit apportionment would be a problem. With experience, however, the persistent errors and multiple inadequate strategies that would follow from an inadequate goal sketch would trigger revision of the goal sketch itself. Thus, goal sketches and the strategies they help generate would interact in a mutually beneficial way.

It is important to note that even perfect goal sketches do not guarantee that successful strategies will be generated. They cannot even guarantee that flawed strategies will not be generated. Flawed strategies can emerge, for example, in situations in which an answer must be produced and no procedure is available for meeting the goals in the goal sketch. The "buggy" subtraction algorithms described by Brown and VanLehn (1980) present one such example. Many children can correctly solve long subtraction problems except when the problem demands borrowing across a zero (e.g., $703 - 567$). Such problems elicit a variety of specific errors, such as subtracting 0 from 6 instead of 6 from 0 and failing to reduce the number of hundreds after borrowing. These flawed strategies seem unlikely to reflect absence of knowledge of relevant goals. In protocol studies, when children are presented problems in which they need to borrow across a zero, they often explicitly state that they do not know how to solve the problem. Only when the experimenter instructs them to try to solve the problem anyway do these children use buggy strategies (VanLehn, in preparation). As this finding indicates, correct goal sketches are insufficient for generating adequate strategies; procedures that can meet the goals are also necessary.

Even in domains such as simple addition, in which children seem both to know the relevant goals and to possess procedures that can meet them, failure to access the relevant goal structure can lead to unsuccessful performance. This seems especially likely to occur in situations in which children have not had much experience. Consider the following conversation in which the phrasing of the experimenter's question led a 4-year-old boy not to access a goal structure that other evidence suggested he knew:

E: How many is two and one more?

S: Four.

E: Well, how many is two *lollipops* and one more?

S: Three.

E: How many is two *elephants* and one more?

S: Three.

E: How many is two *giraffes* and one more?

S: Three.

E: So, how many is *two* and one more?

S: Six. (Hughes, 1986, pp. 47–48).

Appropriate goal sketches thus help children avoid inappropriate strategies, but do not guarantee against them. Accessing the relevant goal sketch and generating procedures that can meet the goals are also essential for the construction of effective strategies.

Construction of the Min Strategy

The Discovery Process. Having formed a goal sketch of the requirements for a new strategy, children must search existing knowledge for components from which to construct the new approach. One rich source of components is existing strategies for solving the same class of problems. Such strategies must meet many of the same subgoals as a new strategy and therefore include procedures for doing so. For example, if successful strategies in a domain must fulfill two subgoals, a child may create a new strategy for solving problems in that domain by putting together a subroutine from one strategy that meets one subgoal and a subroutine from a second strategy that meets the other subgoal.

Another fertile source of components for constructing new strategies is approaches that have proved useful in related domains. For example, numerical domains other than addition, such as counting and numerical magnitude comparison, would be likely sources of procedures for constructing new addition strategies.

How might such sources help children construct the min strategy? The previous analyses of Neches (1987) and Secada et al. (1983), as well as our own analysis, indicate that accomplishing the following five objectives is essential:

1. Identifying the larger addend;
2. Reversing the addend order if the larger addend is second;
3. Quantitatively representing the larger addend by saying the number used to represent that addend in the original problem;
4. Counting on from the larger addend;
5. Keeping track simultaneously of the running total of counts and of the counts corresponding to the smaller addend, so that counting stops at the right point.

If children needed to master all of these skills at once, they might never discover the min strategy. Such a large leap does not seem essential, though. It appears that four of these five types of knowledge were available to most of the 4- and 5-year-old participants in the present study before the point at which they discovered the min strategy.

First consider identification of the larger addend. The pretest performance of children in this study demonstrated that they could accurately identify the larger of two numbers before they began the experiment.

Next consider reversing the order of the addends. Analyses of children's pauses indicated that seven of the eight children in the study sometimes reversed the order of the addends while executing other strategies, such as the sum or the shortcut-sum approach. When solving 3 + 5, for example, children sometimes counted "1, 2, 3, 4, 5 . . . 6, 7, 8." Thus, this component also did not present any obvious obstacle.

Now consider counting from an arbitrary point greater than one. The present study did not provide directly relevant evidence concerning whether children possessed this skill prior to discovering the min strategy. However, Fuson et al. (1982) found that age peers of the children in the study could usually correctly count on from arbitrary points greater than one. Given that children in the present study were students at a university laboratory school, and that several of them were offspring of university faculty, their knowledge of this and other mathematical skills seemed likely to be at least as advanced as that of children in the more heterogeneous sample tested by Fuson et al.

Children also appeared to master the skill of simultaneously keeping track of two counts before they discovered the min strategy. Such dual monitoring was a necessary part of the shortcut-sum strategy that most children acquired prior to their discovery of the min strategy. The monitoring requirements of the two strategies are identical; in both cases, children must simultaneously keep track of the running total and of whether the count has reached the cardinal value of the addend being counted (e. g., when adding 6 + 3, they could think "7 is 1, 8 is 2, 9 is 3").

The one remaining skill might seem to be the simplest of the five: quantitatively representing the larger addend by repeating the value that was given in the original problem (e. g., in 6 + 3, quantitatively representing 6 by saying "6"). However, Secada et al. (1983) found that many 6- and 7-year-olds who did not know the min strategy also seemed to lack this skill. Also, none of the addition procedures that children in the present experiment used before they discovered the min strategy included quantification of an addend by simply saying the number given in the problem. The absence of evidence that children possessed this component, combined with the evidence for their mastery of the other four components, suggested that ability to quantitatively represent the larger addend by repeating the value used to represent it in the initial problem might be the final obstacle to discovering the min strategy.

If children did not possess this critical piece of knowledge, how might they acquire it? Examining how children executed the strategies they already knew suggests one possible route. As the children in our study gained practice using the sum strategy, they increasingly often represented the value of each addend by putting up that number of fingers without counting them out. For example, asked to solve 4 + 3, they would simply put up 4 fingers without counting "1, 2, 3, 4." In the course of the study, children also became increasingly adept at using finger recognition to identify the number of fingers they held up. On 3 + 1, a child might put up three fingers, put up one more, recognize the combined sets as four, and say "4" without any counting. Combining these two procedures could enable children to understand that an addend can be quantitatively represented by simply repeating its label in the original problem. For example, a child might hear the problem "4 + 3," represent "4" by putting up four fingers, recognize the quantity associated with the four fingers as "4" and say "4" to represent the quantity. The type of composition mechanism described by Lewis (1978) and Neves and Anderson (1981) could be applied to this sequence to eliminate the intermediate procedure of putting up four fingers. This would yield a rule of the form, "If you hear a set described as having N elements, and you want to quantitatively represent the set, then simply say "N." Such a process would yield the missing component.

To summarize, we propose that children as young as 4 and 5 years old can generate goal sketches that indicate the objectives that a legitimate strategy for adding numbers must meet. We further propose that they use such goal sketches to assemble components for new strategies. Procedures within existing addition strategies, knowledge of the goals that these procedures have proved effective in meeting, and information about related domains such as numerical magnitudes all are hypothesized to contribute to discovery of the min strategy.

Generalization. What type of mechanisms might account for children's pattern of generalization of the newly discovered strategy? Such mechanisms would need to simultaneously account for three central phenomena: children's very slow initial adoption of the new strategy; the role of the challenge problems in stimulating use of the new strategy among children who had discovered it earlier; and the tendency of children who were conscious of using the new strategy to subsequently generalize it more broadly. The following are some ideas about mechanisms that might produce these effects.

Children's slow initial uptake of the newly discovered strategy is consistent with the Siegler and Shipley strategy choice model described in chapter 2. On the small-addend problems, which were the only problems presented prior to the challenge set, there was little advantage to using the min strategy. As discussed in chapter 3, the newly discovered min strategy was slightly faster but also slightly less accurate on such problems than the well-established sum strategy. Under such circumstances, the model predicts steady rather than increasing use of a newly acquired strategy.

For children who used the min strategy on the challenge problems, the experience would be expected to lead to more frequent subsequent use of the strategy. Within the Siegler and Shipley model, the much greater speed and accuracy of the min strategy on such problems, relative to the sum and shortcut-sum approaches, would lead to an increased valuation of the min strategy in general and to a lower valuation of alternative approaches. This re-valuation would have led the model, like the children, to subsequently use the min strategy more often on both large- and small-addend problems. The effect would be especially dramatic on problems like 21 + 3, but would be evident on small-addend problems as well.

The other clear influence on amount of generalization of the new strategy was whether the child seemed conscious of the strategy being used. This influence may be due to the effects of consciousness on encoding. One function of consciousness seems to be to create more accessible encodings of both external stimuli and of one's own activities. Problems that present impasses may heighten consciousness (and thereby produce more elaborated encodings) of both the nature of the problems and of procedures that have proved capable of overcoming them. In particular, consciousness may enable people to encode a set of procedures as a distinct strategy useful for achieving a particular goal, rather than as unconnected operations that happened to achieve a goal in one processing episode. In the present situation, the greater use of the min strategy following the challenge problems may have been due to their stimulating an elaborated encoding of the source of the difficulty that such problems posed and also an elaborated encoding of the way in which the strategy overcame the difficulty. Such elaborated encodings could also help children realize the potential advantages of the min strategy on problems where the addends were smaller and less discrepant.

Although this account of discovery and generalization focuses on the min strategy, a number of its features may apply quite generally to strategy construction. The type of framework provided by a goal sketch, indicating the basic goals that any procedure in the particular domain would need to satisfy, seems likely to be broadly useful for directing searches in appropriate directions, and therefore in constructing effective strategies and avoiding inappropriate ones. Existing strategies seems likely to constitute a generally valuable source of procedures from which to build new strategies in the same domain, because they were constructed to meet many of the same goals. The upward re-valuation of occasionally-used strategies when those strategies enable learners to solve problems that present impasses for other strategies also seems likely to occur often. Finally, the role of consciousness, both in creating elaborated initial encodings that make strategies more accessible and in enhancing the encoding of the goals that the strategies have proved useful in meeting, seems likely to be pervasive.

FUTURE OBJECTIVES

The primary goals of this investigation were to develop a conceptual framework for thinking about long-term strategy construction, to identify useful methods for studying it, to uncover empirical phenomena that could constrain theories about it, and to generate hypotheses about underlying mechanisms. The conceptual framework that we developed emphasized a division of the strategy construction process into three phases: the period leading up to discovery of the new strategy, the discovery itself, and the period in which the new strategy is generalized beyond its initial use. Microgenetic methods proved to be useful for studying the strategy construction process and revealed a large number of empirical characteristics of the process that would have been difficult to perceive through use of alternative methods. These observations helped us to formulate ideas about mechanisms, such as the goal sketch.

The results of the study can perhaps best be viewed in terms of the constraints that they place on future models of strategy construction. The constraints were formulated in response to our observations of construction of the min strategy, but they also seem likely to apply to construction of many other strategies. We believe that a satisfactory model should have the following properties:

1. In its initial state, the model should be able to solve problems through use of multiple strategies, but not through the strategy of interest.

2. The model should be capable of discovering the new strategy through experience solving problems in the domain; it should not require external help, such as being given a description of the new strategy or examples of its use, to do so.

3. Immediately prior to the discovery, the amount of cognitive activity should increase in a way that would generate long solution times on these trials.

4. The discovery should not come instantaneously (on the first trial or two of practice) nor should it require thousands of trials; instead, it should occur after a moderate amount of experience.
5. Discoveries should not require an impasse; they should be possible on any problem.
6. It should be possible to create new strategies by detaching from their contexts subroutines that meet goals within existing strategies.
7. Strategies that violate basic goals of the domain should not be attempted.
8. Generalization of the new strategy should proceed slowly as long as the strategy does not produce any great advantage in solving problems.
9. Generalization of the new strategy should increase substantially following presentation of problems on which the new approach is much more effective than alternative approaches.

When we are able to generate a model that simultaneously exhibits these properties, we will have come a long way toward understanding how children construct new strategies in this and, we suspect, many other domains.

References

Anderson, J. R. (1976). *Language, memory, and thought.* Hillsdale, NJ: Lawrence Erlbaum Associates.

Anderson, J. R. (1981). *Cognitive skills and their acquisition.* Hillsdale, NJ: Lawrence Erlbaum Associates.

Anderson, J. R. (1983). *The architecture of cognition.* Cambridge, MA: Harvard University Press.

Anderson, J. R., Greeno, J. G., Kline, P. J., & Neves, D. M. (1981). Acquisition of problem-solving skill. In J. R. Anderson (Ed.), *Cognitive skills and their acquisition* (pp. 191–230). Hillsdale, NJ: Lawrence Erlbaum Associates.

Ashcraft, M. H. (1982). The development of mental arithmetic: A chronometric approach. *Developmental Review, 2,* 213–236.

Ashcraft, M. H. (1987). Children's knowledge of simple arithmetic: A developmental model and simulation. In C. J. Brainerd, R. Kail, & J. Bisanz (Eds.), *Formal methods in developmental psychcology* (pp. 302–338). New York: Springer-Verlag.

Baroody, A. J. (1984). The case of Felicia: A young child's strategies for reducing memory demands during mental addition. *Cognition and Instruction, 1,* 109–116.

Baroody, A. J., & Ginsburg, H. P. (1986). The relationship between initial meaningful and mechanical knowledge of arithmetic. In J. Hiebert (Ed.), *Conceptual and procedural knowledge: The case of mathematics.* (pp. 75–112). Hillsdale, NJ: Lawrence Erlbaum Associates.

Bereiter, C., & Scardamalia, M. (1987). *The psychology of written composition.* Hillsdale, NJ: Lawrence Erlbaum Associates.

Berwick, R. (1985). *The acquisition of syntactic knowledge.* Cambridge, MA: MIT

Press.

Binet, A. (1890). Perceptions d'enfants [Perceptions of children]. *Revue Philosophique, 30,* 582–611.

Bisanz, J., & LeFevre, J. (in press). Strategic and nonstrategic processing in the development of mathematical cognition. In D. Bjorklund (Ed.) *Children strategies: Contemporary views of cognitive development.* Hillsdale, NJ: Lawrence Erlbaum Associates.

Bradley, L., & Bryant, P. E. (1983). Categorizing sounds and learning to read: A causal connection. *Nature, 301,* 419–421.

Brainerd, C. J. (1973). Order of acquisition of transitivity, conservation, and class inclusion of length and weight. *Developmental Psychology, 8,* 105–116.

Brainerd, C. J. (1974). Training and transfer of transitivity, conservation, and class inclusion of length. *Child Development, 45,* 324–344.

Bransford, J. D., & Stein, B. S. (1984). *The ideal problem solver: A guide for improving thinking, learning, and creativity.* New York: Freeman.

Bransford, P. W. (1979). *Human cognition: Learning, understanding and remembering.* Belmont, CA: Wadsworth.

Brown, A. L., & DeLoache, J. S. (1978). Skills, plans, and self-regulation. In R. S. Siegler (Ed.), *Children's thinking: What develops?* (pp. 3–35). Hillsdale, NJ: Lawrence Erlbaum Associates.

Brown, J. S., & VanLehn, K. (1980). Repair theory: A generative theory of bugs in procedural skills. *Cognitive Science, 4,* 379–426.

Brown, R. W. (1956). Language and categories. In J. S. Bruner, J. J. Goodnow, & G. A. Austin (Eds.), *A study of thinking* (pp. 247–312). New York: Wiley.

Bruner, J. S., Goodnow, J. J., & Austin, G. A. (1956). *A study of thinking.* New York: Wiley.

Buckingham, B. R. (1921). Intelligence and its measurement: A symposium. *Journal of Educational Psychology, 12,* 271–275.

Campione, J. C., Brown, A. L., & Bryant, N. R. (1985). Individual differences in learning and memory. In R. J. Sternberg (Ed.), *Human abilities: An information-processing approach* (pp. 103–126). New York: Freeman.

Carpenter, T. P., & Moser, J. M. (1982). The development of addition and subtraction problem solving skills. In T. P. Carpenter, J. M. Moser, & T. A. Romberg (Eds.), *Addition and subtraction: A cognitive perspective* (pp. 9–24). Hillsdale, NJ: Lawrence Erlbaum Associates.

Case, R. (1985). *Intellectual development: Birth to adulthood.* Orlando, FL: Academic Press.

Chase, W. G., & Ericsson, K. A. (1981). Skilled memory. In J. R. Anderson (Ed.), *Cognitive skills and their acquisition* (pp. 141–189). Hillsdale, NJ: Lawrence Erlbaum Associates.

Chase, W. G., & Simon, H. A. (1973). The mind's eye in chess. In W. G. Chase (Ed.), *Visual information processing* (pp. 215–281). New York: Academic Press.

Chi, M. T. H. (1978). Knowledge structures and memory development. In R. S. Siegler (Ed.), *Children's thinking: What develops?* (pp. 73–96). Hillsdale, NJ: Lawrence Erlbaum Associates.

Chipman, S. F., Segal, J. W., & Glaser, R. (1985). *Thinking and learning skills, Vol. 2: Research and open questions.* Hillsdale, NJ: Lawrence Erlbaum Associates.

Collins, A., & Stevens, A. L. (1982). Goals and strategies of inquiry teachers. In R. Glaser (Ed.), *Advances in instructional psychology* (Vol. 2, pp. 65–119). Hillsdale, NJ: Lawrence Erlbaum Associates.

Dearborn, W. G. (1921). Intelligence and its measurement: A symposium. *Journal of Educational Psychology, 12,* 210–212.

Ericsson, K. A., Chase, W. G., & Faloon, S. (1980). Acquisition of a memory skill. *Science, 208,* 1181–1182.

Fitts, P. M., & Posner, M. I. (1967). *Human performance.* Belmont, CA: Brooks/Cole.

Flavell, J. H., & Wohlwill, J. F. (1969). Formal and functional aspects of cognitive development. In D. Elkind & J. H. Flavell (Eds.), *Studies in cognitive development: Essays in honor of Jean Piaget* (pp. 67–120). New York: Oxford University Press.

Fuson, K. C. (1982). An analysis of the counting-on solution procedure in addition. In T. P. Carpenter, J. M. Moser, & T. A. Romberg (Eds.), *Addition and subtraction: A cognitive perspective* (pp. 67–81). Hillsdale, NJ: Lawrence Erlbaum Associates.

Fuson, K. C., Richards, J., & Briars, D. J. (1982). The acquisition and elaboration of the number word sequence. In C. J. Brainerd (Ed.), *Children's logical and mathematical cognition* (pp. 33–92). New York: Springer-Verlag.

Gagne, R. M. (1968). Contributions of learning to human development. *Psychological Review, 75,* 177–191

Geary, D. C., & Burlingham-Dubree, M. in press. External validation of the strategy choice model for addition. *Journal of Experimental Child Psychology.*

Gelman, R. (1969). Conservation acquisition: A problem of learning to attend to relevant attributes. *Journal of Experimental Child Psychology, 7,* 167–187.

Gelman, R., & Gallistel, C. R. (1978). *The child's understanding of number.* Cambridge, MA: Harvard University Press.

Gentner, D., & Toupin, C. (1986). Systematicity and similarity in the development of analogy. *Cognitive Science, 10,* 277–300.

Gholson, B., Levine, M., & Phillips, S. (1972). Hypotheses, strategies, and stereotypes in discrimination learning. *Journal of Experimental Child Psychology, 13,* 423–446.

Giere, R. N. (1988). *Explaining science: A cognitive approach.* Chicago, IL: The University of Chicago Press.

Glaser, R. (1976). Components of a psychology of instruction: Toward a science of design. *Review of Educational Research, 46,* 1–24.

Goldman, S. R., Mertz, D. L., & Pellegrino, J. W. in press. Individual differences in extended practice functions and solution strategies for basic addition facts. *Journal of Educational Psychology.*

Goldman, S. R., Pellegrino, J. W., & Mertz, D. L. (1988). Extended practice of basic addition facts: Strategy changes in learning-disabled students. *Cognition and Instruction, 5,* 223–265.

Gray, B. (1977). *The grammatical foundations of rhetoric.* The Hague, The Netherlands: Mouton Publishers.

Groen, G. J., & Parkman, J. M. (1972). A chronometric analysis of simple addition. *Psychological Review, 79,* 329–343.

Groen, G., & Resnick, L. B. (1977). Can preschool children invent addition algorithms? *Journal of Educational Psychology, 69,* 645–652.

Gruber, H. E. (1981). *Darwin on man: A psychological study of scientific creativity.* Chicago, IL: University of Chicago Press.

Hallam, A. (1975). Alfred Wegener and the hypothesis of continental drift. *Scientific American, 232,* 88–97.

Hanson, N. R. (1961). Is there a logic of discovery? In H. Feigl & G. Maxwell (Eds.), *Current issues in the philosophy of science* (pp. 20–35). New York: Holt, Rinehart & Winston.

Holland, J. H., Holyoak, K. J., Nisbett, R. E., & Thagard, P. R. (1986). *Induction:*

Processes of inference, learning, and discovery. Cambridge, MA: MIT Press.

Huey, E. B. (1908). *The psychology and pedagogy of reading.* Cambridge, MA: MIT Press.

Hughes, M. (1986). *Children and number: Difficulties in learning mathematics.* New York: Basil Blackwell.

Ilg, F., & Ames, L. B. (1951). Developmental trends in arithmetic. *Journal of Genetic Psychology, 79,* 3–28.

Inhelder, B., & Piaget, J. (1958). *The growth of logical thinking from childhood to adolescence.* New York: Basic Books.

Inhelder, B., Sinclair, H., & Bovet, M. (1974). *Learning and the development of cognition.* Cambridge, MA: Harvard University Press.

Johnson-Laird, P. N. (1983). *Mental models.* Cambridge, MA: Harvard University Press.

Kahan, L. D., & Richards, D. D. (1986). The effects of context on children's referential communication strategies. *Child Development, 57,* 1130–1141.

Kail, R. (1984). *The development of memory in children* (2nd ed.). New York: Freeman.

Kaye, D. B., Post, T. A., Hall, V. C., & Dineen, J. T. (1986). The emergence of information retrieval strategies in numerical cognition: A development study. *Cognition and Instruction, 3,* 137–166.

Klahr, D. (1984). Transition processes in quantitative development. In R. J. Sternberg (Ed.), *Mechanisms of cognitive development* (pp. 101–139). New York: Freeman.

Klahr, D., & Carver, S. M. (1988). Cognitive objectives in a LOGO debugging curriculum: Instruction, learning and transfer. *Cognitive Psychology, 20,* 362–404.

Kuhn, D., Amsel, E., & O'Laughlin, M. (1988). *The development of scientific thinking skills.* New York: Academic Press.

Kuhn, D., & Phelps, E. (1982). The development of problem-solving strategies. In H. Reese & L. Lipsitt (Eds.), *Advances in child development and behavior* (Vol. 17, pp. 2–44). New York: Academic Press.

Langley P., Simon, H. A., Bradshaw, G. L. & Zytkow, J. M. (1987). *Scientific discovery.* Cambridge, MA: MIT Press.

Langley, P., Zytkow, J. M., Simon, H. A., & Bradshaw, G. L. (1986). The search for regularity: Four aspects of scientific discovery. In R. S. Michaliski, J. G. Carbonell, & T. M. Mitchell (Eds.), *Machine learning: An artificial intelligence approach* (Vol. 2, pp. 425–470). Los Altos, CA: Morgan Kaufmann.

Lawler, R. W. (1985). *Computer experience and cognitive development: A child's learning in a computer culture.* New York: Wiley.

LeFevre, J., & Bisanz, J. (1986). A cognitive analysis of number-series problems: Sources of individual differences in performance. *Memory and Cognition, 14,* 287–298.

Levine, M. (1966). Hypothesis behavior by humans during discrimination learning. *Journal of Experimental Psychology, 71,* 331–336.

Lewis, C. H. (1978). *Production system models of practice effects.* Unpublished dissertation, University of Michigan at Ann Arbor, Ann Arbor, MI.

MacWhinney, B. (1978). The acquisition of morphophonology. *Monographs of the Society for Research in Child Development, 43* (Whole No. 1).

Maratsos, M. P. (1983). Some current issues in the study of the acquisition of grammar. In J. H. Flavell & E. Markman (Eds.), *Handbook of child psychology* (Vol. 3, pp. 707–786). New York: Wiley.

Markman, E. M. (1978). Empirical versus logical solutions to part-whole comparison problems concerning classes and collections. *Child Development, 49,* 168–177.

Mazur, J., & Hastie, R. (1978). Learning as accumulation: A reexamination of the learning curve. *Psychological Bulletin, 85,* 1256–1274.

McClelland, J. L. (1988). *Parallel distributed processing: Implications for cognition and development* (AIP Technical Report 47). Pittsburgh, PA: Carnegie-Mellon University, Department of Computer Science and Psychology, University of Pittsburgh, Learning Research and Development Center.

McClelland, J. L., & Jenkins, E. (in press). Developmental change: Insights from connectionist models. In K. VanLehn (Ed.), *Architectures for intelligence.* Hillsdale, NJ: Lawrence Erlbaum Associates.

McClelland, J. L., & Rumelhart, D. E. (1986). *Parallel distributed processing: Explorations in the microstructure of cognition.* Cambridge, MA: MIT Press.

McGilly, K., & Siegler, R. S. (1989). How children choose among serial recall strategies. *Child Development, 60,* 172–182.

Metz, K. E. (1985). The development of children's problem solving in a gears task: A problem space perspective. *Cognitive Science, 9,* 431–471.

Miller, G. A., Galanter, E., & Pribram, K. H. (1960). *Plans and the structure of behavior.* New York: Holt, Rinehart & Winston.

National Assessment of Educational Progress. (1983). *The third national mathematics assessment: Results, trends, and issues (13-MA-01).* Denver, CO: Educational Commission of States.

Neches, R. (1987). Learning through incremental refinement procedures. In D. Klahr, P. Langley, & R. Neches (Eds.), *Production system models of learning and development* (pp. 163–219). Cambridge, MA: MIT Press.

Neves, D. M., & Anderson, J. R. (1981). Knowledge compilation: Mechanisms for the automatization for cognitive skills. In J. R. Anderson (Ed.), *Cognitive skills and their acquisition* (pp. 57–84). Hillsdale, NJ: Lawrence Erlbaum Associates.

Newell, A. (in press). *Unified theories of cognition: The William James Lectures.* Cambridge, MA: Harvard University Press.

Newell, A., & Rosenbloom, P. S. (1981). Mechanisms of skill acquisition and the law of practice. In J. R. Anderson (Ed.), *Cognitive skills and their acquisition* (pp. 1–55). Hillsdale, NJ: Lawrence Erlbaum Associates.

Newell, A., & Simon, H. A. (1956). The logic theory machine: A complex information processing system. *IRE transactions on information theory, Vol. IT-2, No. 3,* 61–79.

Newell, A., & Simon, H. A. (1972). *Human problem solving.* Englewood Cliffs, NJ: Prentice-Hall.

Nickles, T. (1978). *Scientific discovery: Case studies.* Dordrecht: Reidel.

Nisbett, R. E., & Wilson, T. D. (1977). Telling more than we can know: Verbal reports on mental processes. *Psychological Review, 84,* 231–259.

O'Sullivan, J. T., & Pressley, M. (1984). Completeness of instruction and strategy transfer. *Journal of Experimental Child Psychology, 38,* 275–288.

Palincsar, A. S., & Brown, A. L. (1984). Reciprocal teaching of comprehension-monitoring activities. *Cognition and Instruction, 1,* 117–175.

Paris, S. G., Newman, R. S., & McVey, K. A. (1982). Learning the functional significance of mnemonic actions: A microgenetic study of strategy acquisition. *Journal of Experimental Child Psychology, 34,* 490–509.

Payne, J. W. (1976). Task complexity and contingent processing in decision making: An information search and protocol analysis. *Organizational Behavior and Human Performance, 16,* 366–387.

Payne, J. W., Bettman, J. R., & Johnson, E. J. (1988). Adaptive strategy selection in decision making. *Journal of Experimental Psychology: Learning, Memory, and Cognition, 14* 534-552.

Piaget, J. (1970). *Psychology and epistemology.* New York: W. W. Norton.

Popper, K. (1959). *The logic of scientific discovery.* New York: Basic Books.

Reder, L. (1987). Strategy selection in question answering. *Cognitive Psychology, 19,* 90-138.

Reed, S. K., Ernst, G. W., & Banerji, R. (1974). The role of analogy in transfer between similar problem states. *Cognitive Psychology, 6,* 436-450.

Resnick, L. B. & Neches, R. (1984). Factors affecting individual differences in learning ability. In R. J. Sternberg (Ed.), *Advances in the psychology of human intelligence* Vol. 2 pp. 275-323. Hillsdale, NJ: Lawrence Erlbaum Associates.

Richards, D. D. (1982). Children's time concepts: Going the distance. In W. J. Friedman (Ed.), *The developmental psychology of time* (pp. 13-45). New York: Academic Press.

Rosenbloom, P. S., & Newell, A. (1986). The chunking of goal hierarchies: A generalized model of practice. In R. S. Michalski, J. G. Carbonell, & T. M. Mitchell (Eds.), *Machine learning: An artificial intelligence approach* (Vol. 2, pp. 247-288). Los Altos, CA: Kaufmann.

Schauble, L. (1989). *Processes of constructive learning and inference in children: Understanding the causal structure of a microworld.* Unpublished manuscript.

Schoenfeld, A. H. (1987). *Cognitive science and mathematics education.* Hillsdale, NJ: Lawrence Erlbaum Associates.

Scholnick, E. K., & Friedman, S. L. (1987). The planning construct in the psychological literature. In S. L. Friedman, E. K. Scholnick, & R. R. Cocking (Eds.), *Blueprints for thinking* (pp. 3-38). New York: Cambridge University Press.

Secada, W. G., Fuson, K. C., & Hall, J. W. (1983). The transition from counting-all to counting-on in addition. *Journal for Research in Mathematics Education, 14,* 47-57.

Shultz, T. R., Fisher, G. W., Pratt, C. C., & Rulf, S. (1986). Selection of causal rules. *Child Development, 57,* 143-152.

Siegler, R. S. (1976). Three aspects of cognitive development. *Cognitive Psychology, 8,* 481-520.

Siegler, R. S. (1978). The origins of scientific reasoning. In R. S. Siegler (Ed.), *Children's thinking: What develops?* (pp. 109-149). Hillsdale, NJ: Lawrence Erlbaum Associates.

Siegler, R. S. (1981). Developmental sequences within and between concepts. *Monographs of the Society for Research in Child Development, 46,* 1-74.

Siegler, R. S. (1983). Five generalizations about cognitive development. *American Psychologist, 38,* 263-277.

Siegler, R. S. (1986). Unities in strategy choices across domains. In M. Perlmutter (Ed.), *Minnesota symposium on child development* (Vol. 19, pp. 1-48). Hillsdale, NJ: Lawrence Erlbaum Associates.

Siegler, R. S. (1987a). Strategy choices in subtraction. In J. Sloboda & D. Rogers (Eds.), *Cognitive process in mathematics* (pp. 81-106). Oxford: Oxford University Press.

Siegler, R. S. (1987b). The perils of averaging data over strategies: An example from children's addition. *Journal of Experimental Psychology: General, 116,* 250-264.

Siegler, R. S. (1988a). Strategy choice procedures and the development of multiplication skill. *Journal of Experimental Psychology: General, 117,* 258-275.

Siegler, R. S. (1988b). Individual differences in strategy choices: Good students, not-so-good students, and perfectionists. *Child Development, 59,* 833–851.

Siegler, R. S., & McGilly, K. (1989). Strategy choices in children's time-telling. In I. Levin & D. Zakai (Eds.), *Psychological time: A life span perspective.* Elsevier: The Netherlands.

Siegler, R. S., & Richards, (1979). Development of time, speed, and distance concepts. *Developmental Psychology, 15,* 288–298.

Siegler, R. S. (in press). The hazards of mental chronometry: An example from children's subtraction. *Journal of Educational Psychology.*

Siegler, R. S., & Robinson, M. (1982). The development of numerical understandings. In H. Reese & L. P. Lipsitt (Eds.), *Advances in child development and behavior* (Vol. 16, pp. 241–312). New York: Academic Press.

Siegler, R. S., & Shrager, J. (1984). A model of strategy choice. In C. Sophian (Ed.), *Origins of cognitive skills* (pp. 229–293). Hillsdale, NJ: Lawrence Erlbaum Associates.

Simon, H. A., & Hayes, J. R. (1976). Understanding complex task instructions. In D. Klahr (Ed.), *Cognition and instruction* (pp. 269–285). Hillsdale, NJ: Lawrence Erlbaum Associates.

Staszewski, J. (1987). *Psychological reality of retrieval structures.* Unpublished doctoral dissertation, Cornell University, Ithaca, NY.

Staszewski, J. (1988). Skilled memory and expert mental calculation. In M. T. H. Chi, R. Glaser, & M. J. Farr (Eds.), *The nature of expertise* (pp. 71–128). Hillsdale, NJ: Lawrence Erlbaum Associates.

Sternberg, R. J. (1985). *Beyond IQ: A triarchic theory of human intelligence.* New York: Cambridge University Press.

Stevenson, H. (1983). How children learn: The quest for a theory. In W. Kessen (Ed.), *Handbook of child psychology* (Vol. 1, pp. 213–236). New York: Wiley.

Svenson, O. (1975). Analysis of time required by children for simple additions. *Acta Psychologica, 39,* 289–302.

Svenson, O. & Broquist, S. (1975). Strategies for solving simple addition problems: A comparison of normal and subnormal children. *Scandinavian Journal of Psychology, 16,* 143–151.

Thorndike, E. L. (1903). *Educational psychology.* New York: Lemcke & Buechner.

VanLehn, K. (1988). Towards a theory of impasse-driven learning. In H. Mandl & A. Lesgold (Eds.), *Learning issues for intelligent tutoring systems.* New York: Springer.

VanLehn, K. (in preparation). *Tutorial instruction need not obey felicity conditions on lesson scope and sequence.*

Voss, J. F. (1978). Cognition and instruction: Toward a cognitive theory of learning. In A. M. Lesgold, J. W. Pellegrino, S. D. Fokkema, & R. Glaser (Eds.), *Cognitive psychology and instruction* (pp. 13–26). New York: Plenum Press.

Wegener, A. (1966). *The origin of continents and oceans* (J. Biram, trans.). New York: Dover. (Originally published 1929).

Woodrow, H. (1921). What I conceive intelligence to be. *Journal of Educational Psychology, 12,* 205–210.

Author Index

Subject Index